D1616140

Protestants and Catholics

A Guide to Understanding the Differences among Christians

Peter Toon

SERVANT BOOKS
Ann Arbor, Michigan

Copyright © 1983 by Peter Toon
All rights reserved

First American edition 1984 by:
    Servant Books
    P.O. Box 8617
    Ann Arbor, Michigan 48107

First published 1983 by:
Marshall Morgan and Scott

Cover design by John B. Leidy
Cover photos by Michael Andaloro, John Leidy,
Gerry Rauch   © 1984 Servant Publications

84 85 86 10 9 8 7 6 5 4 3 2 1

Printed in the United States of America
ISBN 0-89283-188-X

Contents

This book is dedicated to the
Reverend Theodore A. McConnell,
Anglican priest in Warrensburg,
New York, who has shown me great
kindness, and who longs for greater
unity among Christians.

Preface

I began to think about writing this book during discussions about the implications of the visit of the Pope to Great Britain in May 1982. I thank John Hunt of Marshall Morgan & Scott for inviting me to proceed.

My thinking on various difficult areas has been helpfully clarified through discussion with several Roman Catholic theologians. I sincerely hope that I have faithfully recorded what the Roman Catholic Church teaches, but in order to give an authoritative summary I have included as an appendix the profession of faith made by Pope Paul VI on 30 June 1968, on the nineteenth centenary of the martyrdom of the apostles Peter and Paul.

The readership I have had in mind while writing is the whole English-speaking world, and in particular those whom I may call orthodox, evangelical or traditional Protestants. I have included as an appendix the statement of faith known as the *Lausanne Covenant* (1974), one of the few exciting professions of faith to be produced by Protestants in modern times. It must be remembered that this statement of faith is not that of any single Protestant Church, but was produced by representative evangelical Protestants from many parts of the world.

Two further appendices contain the three 'Catholic' creeds, and a remarkable *Letter to a Roman Catholic* written by John Wesley to Irish Roman Catholic laity in 1739.

For the official texts I quote, I have used a variety of sources and translations. These are listed in the bibliography.

The book was written during my summer vacation, as I moved from a house on the campus of Oak Hill College,

London, to a rectory in the quiet and pretty countryside of Suffolk. I am no longer a tutor in a theological college; I now assist a diocesan bishop in the training of younger clergy.

I have found, through working on this book, a greater understanding both of Roman Catholicism, and of Protestantism. I sincerely hope that its readers will have a similar experience.

Peter Toon
24 August 1982

The Rectory
Boxford, Suffolk

Additional Note

I feel honored that an American edition is being published in 1984. In particular I am most happy that this is by Servant Publications because of its association with The Word of God community and its commitment to genuine unity.

May I also say that since the British edition appeared in May 1983 there has appeared in the U.S.A. my book *Justification and Sanctification* (Crossway Publications, Westchester, Illinois), which treats in depth the subject of chapter six in this book.

The genuine unity I look for is a unity in and with diversity, not unity in uniformity.

Advent 1983

Introduction

This book is mainly written for orthodox Protestants who see themselves as maintaining the basic insights and doctrines of the Protestant reformers of the sixteenth and seventeenth centuries — though often expressing them in the language and terminology of the twentieth century. It is a book written from within the Protestant tradition, a tradition which includes faithfulness to the gospel as it is presented in the Bible and a genuine concern for catholicity and continuity with the past. Liberal Protestants, if they recognise the presuppositions with which I am working, will possibly find the book helpful or interesting; Roman Catholics may also find it useful as an attempt to present the doctrinal differences between their communion and Protestantism in an objective and just way. I hope that they will feel I have treated their position sensitively and fairly.

I must emphasise that this is not a book about religious personalities. It contains no critical comments about any Pope, Jesuit or Irish priest. Neither is it concerned with the way human relationships work at the local and personal level — most of us have friends or acquaintances who are Roman Catholics and we value their friendship and support. We know that Roman Catholic neighbours are no better or worse neighbours than Protestant ones.

It is so easy to typecast. Here is an American version of one way in which Roman Catholics sometimes 'stereotype' Protestants:

Protestants are responsible for disrupting the unity of the church founded by Jesus Christ. In refusing to give their allegiance to the vicar of Christ, sixteenth-century Protestants created new sects founded by man rather than God. Protestants continue to do the same thing, whether the founder in question is Luther or Calvin or Henry VIII or Joseph Smith or Aimée Semple Macpherson. As a result, it is difficult to know what Protestants believe, because they have always disagreed among themselves, and start new churches if the disagreements get too violent. About all they really believe in common is that the extension of Roman Catholicism must be stopped by whatever means are necessary.

Protestants talk a great deal about tolerance, but they are intolerant of Roman Catholics who run for public office, and of Roman Catholic parents who want to give their children a Christian education by sending them to parochial schools.

And here, from the same continent, is a Protestant stereotype of Roman Catholicism:

Roman Catholicism is a rigid, authoritarian system, much like Communism. Everything is decided by the Pope. All other Roman Catholics have to believe what they are told. They believe that the sacraments are magic and that all non-Catholics are going to hell. They perpetuate this kind of brainwashing through parochial schools, whose purpose is to keep Roman Catholics ignorant of the truth so that they will believe whatever the priest tells them.

Roman Catholics want to dominate the world. When they get enough power they will force everybody to believe as they believe. Since they don't have a democratic church, Roman Catholics don't believe in democracy, and Roman Catholics who say they do will be tolerated only so long as they are in a minority.

If you live in the United Kingdom, especially in Northern Ireland, you will be aware of similar views regularly aired on both sides.

This book is about the teaching (or 'doctrine') within the Roman Catholic and the Protestant communities. I shall not be dealing with the personal views of any archbishop, politician or professor, however well-known. I do not doubt that such opinions are interesting, but I will leave them for other books and the media, and concern myself with comparing what may be called the 'official and traditional' teaching of each community.

One thing that is immediately obvious is that it is much easier to state Roman Catholic teaching than it is to state Protestant teaching. The reason is that we are comparing, not two communities, but one large community and a collection of related, but not united, communities — Protestantism, which includes Presbyterians, Lutherans, Anglicans, Baptists and so on. My task is to compare what the Roman Church teaches with what the Protestant churches, insofar as they are in general agreement, teach. And what each side teaches is not to be found in the views of prominent groups and individuals, but in their authoritative, fundamental statements of belief — the creeds, confessions of faith, synodical declarations and so on.

Some people today might disagree, arguing that these statements are in general out of date and believed only by a minority. If that is so then it is high time that what is officially declared as true should be made to match what is generally believed to be true. But until that happens, we have to work from what officially exists and what has not been officially denied. And that we find in the doctrinal statements.

I have no desire whatsoever to increase bigotry and intolerance. At the same time, I do not want to pretend that major differences do not exist, or that such differences should not be taken seriously. What I want to do is to point out where the differences lie, so that they can be taken seriously in the relationship between Roman Catholic and Protestant Churches.

At the same time, however, I want to insist that to take

our differences seriously does not mean to reject each other's fundamental personhood and rights. In the final analysis, what is much more important than our differences is the fact that we are human beings who look to the God and Father of our Lord Jesus Christ as our Saviour.

1: Clearing the deck

Certain widely-held misunderstandings should be got rid of at the outset.

1. The pilgrim Protestant church

It is often suggested that a pure — or even relatively pure — 'Protestant-type' church survived, outside the Latin Church, through the 'Dark' and 'Middle' Ages into the sixteenth century where it emerged as Protestantism. But in reality, there was no such thing. It is true that interesting groups did exist, like the Albigensians in Languedoc and the Waldensians who emerged as a twelfth-century movement and later became a Protestant denomination. It's true that there were Lollards in England from the fourteenth to sixteenth centuries and Hussites in Bohemia in the fifteenth century — both of them were reforming groups, wanting to restore primitive Christianity but lacking the means to do so. But serious study of history provides no solid evidence of an 'evangelical' church or groups — a 'pilgrim' or 'Bible-based church' — with a continuing existence outside the great catholic Latin patristic and mediaeval Church of Western Europe.

What we do find is that the Christian Church in Western Europe was bound legally and doctrinally to the Bishop of Rome, who was considered to be the head of the Church on earth. And in this large body, from time to time and in various places, certain people and various groups arose, voiced criticism of accepted doctrine and practice, and called for change. By the standards of later Protestantism, hardly any of these groups could be called 'orthodox'.

11

It is better to think of the Western Catholic Church as a Church in which it was possible both to reach great heights of communion with God (for example, think of the hymns of St. Bernard, still sung today by Protestants) — and also to distort the gospel of grace into a system of trying to please God through religious rites and good behaviour. It was the Church of God: but it contained certain features which needed correction and certain theological principles which needed changing. It was a massive community in which, beneath an apparent uniformity, there was great variety.

The character and ethos of what came to be called 'Protestantism' were not new phenomena. The reformers believed that they were restoring primitive Christianity. Martin Luther did not intend to cause a schism when in 1517 he began his call for the Church to return to the holy gospel of Christ. His famous *Reformation Treatises* were written in the fervent hope that the whole Church would be reformed by the gospel, under the leading of the Papacy. The rift between Luther and the Pope only happened because of the intransigence of the Pope and his supporters, and their refusal to listen to Luther's call.

The reformers who came later in Germany, Switzerland and Britain, were much more self-conscious about what they were doing. In their own territories they attempted to reform the Church by the Word of God and according to the pattern of primitive Christianity. Unlike the reformers of the Middle Ages, those of the sixteenth century had many advantages which they used to the full. Not least of these were the support of governments and the availability of printed books. Hence their programme and doctrine were more far-reaching than was ever possible for earlier would-be reformers of the Church.

2. What does 'Protestant' mean?

A second misunderstanding is that the word 'Protestant' means 'somebody who protests against the errors of the Roman Catholic Church'. It is often used in that sense, but the Latin word from which it comes means first of all 'to declare something formally in public, to testify, to make a solemn declaration'. The connotation of 'protesting against error' is only a secondary meaning.

The original 'Protestants' were people in the German town of Spires. In 1529 they made a solemn **Protestation** on behalf of the evangelical cause in Europe. The Pope and the Holy Roman Emperor were attempting to stamp out the new evangelical teaching by use of secular power; it looked like being a fight to the death. So the supporters of the evangelical cause, the 'Protestants', declared:

> There is, we affirm, no sure preaching or doctrine but that which abides by the Word of God. According to God's command no other doctrine should be preached. Each text of the holy and divine scriptures should be elucidated and explained by other texts. This Holy Book is in all things necessary for the Christian; it shines clearly in its own light, and is found to enlighten the darkness. We are determined by God's grace and aid to abide by God's Word alone, the Holy Gospel contained in the biblical books of the Old and New Testaments. This Word alone should be preached, and nothing that is contrary to it. It is the only Truth. It is the sure rule of all Christian doctrine and conduct. It can never fail us or deceive us. Whoso builds and abides on this foundation shall stand against all the gates of hell, while all merely human additions and vanities set up against it must fall before the presence of God.

The *Protestation* is a powerful declaration of faithfulness to the gospel of our Lord Jesus Christ, recorded in the Bible and to be preached in the power of the Holy Spirit; to be a 'Protestant' is to declare an allegiance to our Lord Jesus Christ as he is presented in the words of the Bible. Therefore (as somebody has aptly remarked), the word 'Protestant' is not a word to be forgotten, but a word to be understood.

It would be foolish to assert that there were no negative ideas implicit in the early use of the word. Of course those who used it used it to criticise the existing Church, with its thick veneer of traditions which hid the gospel from sight. And of course it did imply also the possibility that a Church could exist which was not under papal domination and was not overlaid with human tradition. Nevertheless, the primary meaning of the word is positive. To be a Protestant is to be positively in favour of the gospel of God concerning Jesus Christ our Lord, and to seek to implement the principles and purity of the primitive Church.

3. The origins of the great national Protestant Churches of Europe

A third misunderstanding is that the great Protestant national Churches of England, Scotland, Germany, Scandinavia and some of the Swiss cantons were new denominations created in the sixteenth century as a result of the teaching of Luther, Calvin and others. They were not. The Church that had been in existence in those countries for centuries was reformed and continued. There was no break in the weekly worship of parish congregations. People did not stop being Christians during the time they changed their loyalties. Instead, the link with Rome was broken and the liturgy, doctrine and canon law were reformed locally. The reform took place within the continuing life and structure of the Church, and the possibility of it doing so existed because the Head of State or government in each case either supported, or called for, the changes. The reformers saw what they were doing as 'a washing of the dirty face of the Church', as renewal. They believed that what they were doing was to preserve the purity of the one, holy, catholic and apostolic church as it was found in their own territory and country.

Visible unity was very important to them. They did not tolerate small groups of radical separatists. These —

the Anabaptists (rebaptisers) and radical reformers — wanted even more extended reform, by totally separating Church and State, and ensuring that each church was a fellowship of believers. By contrast, reformers like John Calvin attempted to preserve the reality of a State Church (or *Volkskirche*), while at the same time working to make it into a true fellowship of believing Christians (a *Bekenntniskirche*).

In these countries the results of the help given by the civil government can still be seen. For example, in England the monarch is still the nominal 'supreme governor of the Church of England', and in the Scandinavian countries the governments collect a church tax and pay the salaries of the parish clergy.

Most modern denominations have their roots in one or other of these national churches which assumed a Protestant identity in the sixteenth century. In America, for example, the major Presbyterian Churches trace their origins to the Church of Scotland, and the big Lutheran Churches trace theirs to both the German and Scandinavian national Churches. In England, Methodism grew from the Church of England; many of the large Baptist Churches began by conscious separation from national Churches (eg the Anglican Church) in the seventeenth century.

4. Agreements and disagreements

Contrary to what is often thought, there were large areas of agreement between the Protestant national Churches and those parts of the mediaeval Latin Church which remained loyal to the Bishop of Rome (and thereby became what we now call 'Roman Catholicism', or the Roman Catholic Church). It was the intense commitment of both sides to the things on which they differed, which drove them further apart.

The most obvious areas of agreement were the three

traditional creeds of Western Christendom. The *Apostles'*
Creed found its way into many Protestant catechisms,
because it was a basic summary of the facts of Christianity. The longer and more 'theological' *Nicene Creed*
(produced by the Councils of Nicea and Constantinople)
found its way into confessions of faith and the text of the
liturgy of Holy Communion. The *Athanasian Creed*
('Quicunque vult') was incorporated into certain forms of
worship such as Morning Prayer in the Church of
England, and it also became the basis for doctrinal
statements in the confessions of faith.

What the use of these creeds indicates is that there was
a fundamental agreement in Christendom, as to the
doctrines of the Holy Trinity (that God is One yet also
Three in One), and the doctrine of the person of Christ
(that he is one person with two natures, both human and
divine). That is why both Roman Catholics and Protestants bitterly opposed the teaching known as Socinian-
ism, which denied the doctrine of the Trinity.

Another obvious area of agreement was in the status
given to the sixty-six books of the Bible. Both believed
that the Bible was truly God's Word, its authors having
been inspired by the Holy Spirit. Therefore it had divine
authority for faith and morals. The differences arose over
the use and interpretation of the Bible.

There was agreement, too, about the fact that it was
God's will that his church on earth should have visible
unity. The differences lay in how the unity was to be
established and maintained.

In our modern age, when those who take Christianity
seriously are a minority within Western society, we do
not have quite the same view of the sixteenth century as
did our forefathers who lived then. For many people
today the predominant impression is of two groups with
much in common, disagreeing over matters which were
important but not primary. To our forefathers, who
accepted without question the fact of basic agreement
over fundamental doctrines, the differences seemed to

16

them to concern primary issues. To those involved in the struggles of the sixteenth-century Church, they were differences worth dying for. What we see is — at least in part — determined by where we stand.

5. A developing teaching

It is a mistake to think that the 'Calvinists' and 'Lutherans' of later centuries necessarily taught the same things as the reformers whose names they bear. That may seem an obvious point; but it is one worth making. The first reformers handed down principles, doctrines, suggestions and examples to their colleagues and later followers. Because they were not robots, their followers adapted and developed the teaching they received. Circumstances changed; controversy came; new needs, new problems arose; and so the received teaching expanded or contracted, withered or blossomed, to meet the needs of the time.

For example, the teaching of the 1618 Reformed Synod of Dordt is often called 'Calvinist'. The 'five canons' of this Synod comprised a developed form of the doctrines of predestination, atonement and the response of sinners to the gospel which Calvin had taught in Geneva. It is debatable whether or not he would have agreed with the way that the Synod expressed them. Indeed, historians disagree as to whether the theologians of the seventeenth century Reformed Churches remained faithful to Calvin's basic teaching.

But if we go on into the nineteenth century, we find the word 'Calvinist' being stretched to include positions which Calvin specifically opposed! Take Charles Haddon Spurgeon, the gifted and eloquent Baptist preacher. He disagreed with Calvin's teaching on basic matters like baptism, the nature of the church, and the relationship of Church and State. But he is often called a Calvinist; he himself was happy to accept the title. What unites Calvin and Spurgeon is a similar doctrine of the sovereignty of God in salvation, and a historical line of descent which stretches from the Marian exiles of England (who gave England the Geneva Bible in 1560) into English Puritanism and, eventually, Protestant Nonconformity or Dissent. Spurgeon was a Dissenter or Nonconformist.

In the same way, much Lutheran theology and practice in the decades and centuries after Luther's death has been such that it is questionable whether Luther himself could have accepted it. In Lutheran orthodoxy of the seventeenth century for example, and in Lutheran Pietism of the eighteenth and nineteenth centuries, justification and sanctification were carefully distinguished as two separate (though related) acts of God for the sinner. Those who know Luther's writings know that he did not make such a distinction, but actually included the one in the other. Furthermore, Luther's hard doctrine of predestination and strong belief in the bondage of the human will to sin were softened by those who followed him.

As a teacher, I have often found that students believe that their own evangelical views and principles are the same as those of whoever their favourite or 'denominational' reformer is. When they actually study the writings of Calvin and Luther seriously, many are surprised and shocked. Fortunately their surprise is positive, because what they have discovered is a richer source of theology and worship than what they had previously thought to be the Protestant tradition.

6. The reform of Rome

The last misunderstanding that should be discarded is that the Roman Catholic Church is an unreformed Church. In fact, it responded to the loss of large parts of the mediaeval Church by undertaking a certain amount of internal reform. This movement is called the 'Counter-Reformation'.

In the monasteries and the monastic orders, there was reform and renewal. The ideals of chastity, celibacy and selfsacrifice were taught and exemplified. New orders were founded, the most important being the Society of Jesus (the Jesuits) in 1540. Led by Ignatius Loyola and Francis Xavier, the Society became important both in educating European Roman Catholics and in pioneering missionary work overseas.

The famous Council of Trent (1545–1563) restated doctrine and strengthened the discipline of the Church. The Council established Roman Catholic doctrine as something distinct from Protestant doctrine, and it demanded the reform of many aspects of church life.

Also, changes were made within the Vatican at Rome, where the Pope lived and his curia (the government departments) flourished.

By the 1560s, the results of this counter-reformation were being felt. Roman Catholicism had recovered from the blows dealt by the Protestant reformers, and was seeking to stand firm on its basis of a renewed western mediaeval Christianity. It was also regaining territory, and finding vast new territories abroad as the Spanish and Portuguese empires expanded.

*　　*　　*　　*

I am writing primarily for Protestants, and so I have referred to Protestant misunderstandings. Were I writing primarily for Roman Catholics, I would refer to different misunderstandings: for example, the belief of many Roman Catholics that Protestants do not really believe that Christ is present in the Lord's Supper (the Eucharist, or Holy Communion). With few exceptions, Protestants of the sixteenth century did believe that Christ really was present. But they explained that holy presence in a different way to Roman Catholics.

Hopefully, we have begun to clear the decks. Next, we must establish what may be called the credentials of each side.

2: Establishing credentials

There was one Church in Europe when the sixteenth century began. Each nation's Church and that of each empire was under the jurisdiction of the bishop of Rome, the universal pastor. When the century ended, there were in Europe the Roman Catholic Church, which still regarded the Pope as universal pastor, and the Protestant national Churches, which did not. Doctrine and ecclesiastical loyalties no longer united Christendom. Earlier, there had been a schism between eastern and western Christendom. Now western Christendom itself was divided.

Today, the European situation has not altered very much (apart from the general present-day lack of interest in religion and the fact that Protestantism now expresses itself not only in the national Churches but also in denominations such as the Baptists, Methodists and so on). European Christendom is still divided.

As Roman Catholic and Protestant missionary activities have progressed, the labels and divisions of European Christianity have been transported to Asia, Africa, America and Australasia. As might be expected, new forms of the Church have grown up in those continents, precisely because of the polarising tendency which seems to characterise dynamic Protestantism. Nevertheless, there are prominent features of most modern forms of Protestantism which can be traced back to sixteenth-century principles and doctrines: the authority of the Bible, the question of whose right it is to read and interpret it, and the claim that the great message of the Bible is salvation through grace and by faith.

If western Christendom was (and is) divided in this way,

where do the Roman Catholics and Protestants find the doctrines on which they differ? Of course both claim that their source of doctrine is the Bible. But, as we shall see, they both use the Bible differently. In this chapter we will examine their authoritative statements of belief, which both sides claim to be Bible-based. (It should be remembered, in this context, that while both accept the sixty-six books of the Bible, Roman Catholics in addition accept the eight Greek Books of the Apocrypha as Holy Scripture.)

Roman Catholic teaching

Official Roman Catholic teaching means teaching approved by an ecumenical council (a convocation of bishops and their advisers), or declared by the Pope when he speaks infallibly on behalf of the universal Church. We shall look at each of these in more detail.

There have been, according to Roman Catholic belief, twenty-one ecumenical (which means 'worldwide') councils. The Eastern Orthodox Churches recognise only the first seven as truly ecumenical, and consider the last fourteen to be 'western councils', called by the Pope.

A list of the councils is given in Appendix 5. The last three (the Council of Trent, 1545–63; Vatican I, 1868–70; and Vatican II, 1962–65) are of particular importance because they took place after the division of western Christendom. We shall turn to these often for information about Roman Catholic beliefs.

The view of the bishop of Rome as universal pastor led naturally to the Roman Catholic belief that he is able to interpret the Christian faith authoritatively. When there is debate over what the Christian position is on a subject, or what a doctrine means in practice, he speaks to lead the Church in knowledge and understanding. However, his pronouncements are not all made at the same level of authority. The Encyclical Letters (the 'Encyclicals') sent by the Pope to the bishops and through them to all the faithful, represent authoritative interpretations or confirmations of the faith already held. They do not attempt to define new doctrine, but merely to state the meaning and implications of what is already believed. On the other hand, there are rare occasions when the Pope does make a statement in a 'Bull' (the most solemn and weighty form of Papal Letter) or an 'Apostolic Constitution'; this represents a development of doctrine or a new dogma — that is, doctrinal teaching — which the whole Church must believe. Two examples are Pope Pius IX's proclamation of the dogma of the Immaculate Conception of the Blessed Virgin Mary (1854), and Pope Pius XII's proclamation in 1950 of the dogma of the Assumption of the Blessed Virgin Mary. (The content of these dogmas will be discussed in a later chapter.)

Protestant teaching

Each national Church or denomination within Protestantism has its own statement of doctrine. Virtually all accept the basic dogmas of the first four ecumenical councils. So they agree with Roman Catholicism on the fundamental doctrines of the Holy Trinity and of Jesus Christ as one Person but truly God and truly man, and that teaching is found both in their Confessions of Faith and in the use of the Nicene Creed in worship services.

What unites the Protestant statements of faith is the claim to represent the primitive teaching of Holy Scripture, and the insistence that salvation depends on God's grace and is obtained by faith without reference to any human merit. Since Protestantism is a very varied phenomenon we will not attempt to examine it in detail; instead we will look at the doctrinal bases of five groups — Lutherans, Presbyterians, Anglicans, Methodists and Baptists.

Lutherans

There are large Lutheran, or Evangelical, Churches in the States of Germany, in the countries of Scandinavia and in North America. There are also younger Lutheran

Churches in places where Lutheran missions have operated. The Lutheran World Federation was founded in 1947. Its Constitution expresses the basis of Lutheranism:

> The Lutheran World Federation acknowledges the Holy Scriptures of the Old and New Testaments as the only source and the infallible norm of all church doctrine and practice, and sees in the three Ecumenical creeds (Apostles', Nicene and Athanasian) and in the Confessions of the Lutheran Church, especially in the unaltered *Augsburg Confession* and Luther's *Small Catechism*, a pure exposition of the Word of God.

The Augsburg Confession (1530) and Luther's *Small Catechism* (1529) are early statements of doctrine, as are the *Large Catechism* (1529) and the *Schmalkaldic Articles* (1537), also composed by Martin Luther who hoped to present them to a General Council of the Church. (The *Apology for the Augsburg Confession* (1531) and the *Formula of Concord* (1577) should also be mentioned). The various Lutheran doctrinal statements were collected in the *Book of Concord* (1580), but this book is not accepted by all the Lutheran Churches.

Presbyterians
The name comes from 'presbyter', and refers to local churches governed by 'presbyters' (a Greek word meaning 'elders'). These local churches are joined together in presbyteries (presbyters from all the parishes in a given geographical area). 'Presbyterianism' is a general title given to the Englishspeaking reformed Churches, who trace their theological emphases to Calvin's Geneva, and who derive directly or indirectly from the Presbyterian national Church of Scotland. The first reformed Confession of the Church of Scotland was the Calvinist *Scots Confession* (1560). Then in 1648 the *Confession of Faith*, the *Larger* and *Shorter Catechisms*, the *Directory for Public Worship* and the *Form of Government* (all produced at

Westminster Abbey by the famous Westminster Assembly of Divines) were adopted.

In North America the Presbyterian Churches adopted these 'Westminster Standards', as they are called, with minor modifications. Several Churches have added modern confessions, but the intention was not to change the theology of the seventeenth-century statements.

There are other Churches with a presbyterian form of government which are called 'Reformed Churches' — these are found in Switzerland, Holland, France, Germany, South Africa and North America. They make use of one or another of several sixteenth century confessions of faith — for example the *Belgic Confession* (1561), the *French Confession of Faith* (1559), The *Second Helvetic Confession* (1566), and the *Heidelberg Catechism* (1536). There were also earlier confessions which were approved by individual Swiss cantons in the 1530s — the *First Helvetic Confession* (1536), for example, and the *Geneva Confession* (1536). If the Westminster Standards and the continental Confessions are compared, there is a clear family resemblance — the 'head of the family' being John Calvin. These Confessions are concise and easily quoted.

Anglicans
The Anglican Communion of Churches is a worldwide association of Churches which have developed from the Church of England and share a common theology and liturgical tradition with their mother church.

The Church of England was established as a Protestant Church during the reign of Elizabeth I, having undergone reform in the previous reigns. Its theology was expressed in several documents which are still the official statements of faith of the Church of England: *the Thirty-Nine Articles of religion* (1562), the *Book of Homilies* (sermons expounding the Protestant Faith), the *Ordinal* (containing services for the consecration and ordination of bishops, priests and deacons), and the *Book of Common Prayer*, a collection of services for daily, occasional and Sunday use. The last two were revised in

1662. The theology of all these documents is both Protestant and Catholic, in that they demonstrate a genuine desire to hold to the doctrine and practices of the primitive patristic Church.

The Churches of the Anglican Communion have doctrinal bases the same as, or similar to, that of the mother Church. Some of them use the *Lambeth Quadrilateral* (1888), four Articles passed by the American Episcopal Church in 1886. They are brief treatments of Holy Scripture, the Creeds, the two Sacraments and the order of bishops. In addition each Church has its own liturgy, parts of which sometimes indicate minor departures from authentic Protestantism.

It should be added that the declarations made by the Lambeth Conferences, of all Anglican bishops, are not binding on the Churches. They are merely significant expressions of the opinions of the bishops. Each province within the Anglican Communion of Churches is independent of the others. Normally, however, each chooses to cooperate and work with the rest.

Methodists

The name 'Methodist' was originally a nickname, bestowed in 1729 upon a group of serious-minded and disciplined Oxford students. One of them, John Wesley (1703–1791), gave his own definition: 'A Methodist is one who lives according to the method laid down in the Bible.' Methodists were those members of the Church of England who took the call to holiness as a serious call of God. One of the visions that inspired Wesley and his colleagues was that of spreading scriptural holiness throughout the land.

After many years of successful evangelism and of organising converts into 'Societies' loosely connected to the parish churches, Wesley provided in 1784 for the continuance in England, as a corporate body, of what had become known as the 'Yearly Conference of the People called Methodists'. Under a deed poll he nominated some 100 people to be its members and laid down the method of appointing their successors. The Conference was to have charge of the 'Preaching Houses' — the chapels — ownership of which was to be vested in trustees. Wesley provided a 'model trust deed' for the purpose, which stated that the doctrinal basis of preaching in the chapel must agree with the teaching provided in Wesley's *Notes on the New Testament* (1755) and the first four volumes of his sermons (1746–1760) — the 'forty-four sermons'.

The American Methodists were increasing in number. Wesley prepared for them a revision of the Thirty-Nine Articles. The new confession had twenty-five articles. It was adopted at the 1784 Methodist Conference at Baltimore. In 1804 the twenty-third Article was changed to take account of the fact that the USA had become an independent nation.

The doctrinal standard of Methodism, therefore, is essentially the teaching of John Wesley on topics relating to salvation, holiness, evangelism, mission and fellowship; together with the received Catholic doctrine of the Holy Trinity and the Person of Christ, and the Protestant emphasis on the supreme authority of the Scriptures. Wesley interpreted the doctrines of grace, salvation and evangelism in neither Lutheran nor Reformed terms but rather in a similar way to that of Arminius, the Dutch theologian whose views had been condemned by the Synod of Dordt in 1618. In other words, Wesley rejected the Reformed doctrines of predestination, limited atonement and irresistible grace, and instead emphasised the God-given ability of every sinner to respond to the gospel upon hearing it, and so to receive forgiveness of sins and new life in Jesus Christ. This theology is perhaps best known through the hymns of his brother, Charles Wesley.

Soon Methodism was a large and influential denomination in America, and now it — and its offshoots — are to be found all over the world. Because it was itself an offshoot from the Church of England, and because it has always been regarded as receiving its fundamental theology from that Church, Methodism's fundamental confessional basis does not easily lend itself to quotation in a book like this. However, in those areas of doctrine where Protestantism is opposed to Roman Catholicism, the Methodist Churches stand firmly in the Protestant tradition, as is clear in their adoption of the *Twenty-Five Articles*.

Baptists

The name 'Baptists' comes from the practice of baptising those who have made a personal profession of faith in Jesus Christ as Lord and Saviour. In so doing Baptists reject the ancient practice of infant baptism, claiming that it has no scriptural authority. This particular emphasis distinguishes them from the other large Protestant denominations and Churches.

The enormous worldwide family of Baptist Churches has its origins primarily among the Puritans and Separatists in seventeenth century England. Not only did they separate themselves from the parish churches of the national Church, but they also denied that the baptism given to them as infants in that Church was valid. However, when Baptists came into existence there were two schools of thought within Protestantism regarding the correct understanding of the grace of God. One school is referred to as Calvinist or 'Reformed', the other is referred to as Arminian or 'Remonstrant'. Some Baptists adopted a Reformed doctrine of grace, and their theology is expressed in the *Particular Baptist Confession* (1677 and 1689). (The word 'particular' means 'particular redemption' or 'limited atonement' — the doctrine that Christ died only for the elect.) Other Baptists adopted an Arminian position, and their theology is expressed in the *Standard Confession* of 1660. These two schools of thought are to be found among Baptists to this day.

In America, two important Baptist Confessions of Faith were produced. The Philadelphia Confession (1742) is based on the English *Particular Baptist Confession*; its content is thoroughly Calvinistic. The *New*

Hampshire Confession of Faith (1833) attempted to take a middle way between the Arminian and Calvinistic positions with regard to the doctrines of God in salvation. This middle way remains the dominant school of thought on the question of the grace of God.

Baptists of all kinds claim to be under the living Lordship of Christ, and that his Lordship is expressed in the contents of the Holy Scriptures as they are illuminated by the Holy Spirit. The authority of Scripture is clearly stated in all Baptist statements of faith.

How to make comparisons

Comparing Roman Catholicism with Protestantism is not the same as comparing the teaching of one man with another man; it is more like comparing one man's views with those of a group. Sometimes disagreements within a group on certain issues are as strong as their corporate disagreements, on other issues, with their common enemy. Likewise, Protestantism may be regarded as a unity in terms of general ideas and principles — its positive protest — but at the same time, it embraces a variety of apparently irreconcilable views. For example, there is no consensus regarding whether the New Testament allows or commands the practice of infant baptism, nor whether liturgical worship is truly a vehicle of the Holy Spirit or an impediment to his work.

This means that comparison of Roman Catholicism and Protestantism may force us to note differences within Protestantism, and it may well be wise to concede that one criticism Roman Catholics frequently make of Protestants has some weight. They have often pointed out that Protestants, who place great emphasis on the authority and clarity of the Bible, seem unable to agree as to what it actually teaches or even means. It is a criticism that can easily be exaggerated. But Protestants do neither themselves nor their cause any good by vehemently attacking each other and so easily separating from one another.

In our comparison, we shall not rely upon the views of famous theologians or leaders, however significant or famous they may be. To be as objective as possible, we shall rely upon the official statements made by each side. However, because of the unique authority of the Pope within Roman Catholicism, his official statements in Encyclicals will be accepted as authoritative words.

It is not easy to know where to begin. Where, it may be asked, does the basis for the division between Roman Catholics and Protestants lie? In the relationship of the Bible to the accumulated tradition of the historical Church? In the question of authority in the Church, in particular that of the bishop of Rome? In the question of salvation — how is a man justified in the presence of God? Perhaps it lies in all three, and may be in other areas as well.

We have to begin somewhere, however, and we shall begin where the Council of Trent began in 1545: with the topic of tradition.

However, as we all know from personal experience, the significance attached to differences amongst human beings, and the emotion generated by those differences, vary according to the time in which they were discussed. It is pointless to study these differences as if we were still living in the days before the Second Vatican Council. Without doubt, this Council created a new atmosphere in terms of ecumenical relations, and we need to recall and explain this mood before we actually begin to study the major theological differences which certainly still exist.

3: Separated brethren

In a great deal of traditional Protestant theology it has been maintained that the hierarchy, if not the entire membership, of the Roman Church is the fulfilment of the prophecies of Revelation 12–13, and that in particular, the Papacy is the antichrist. On the other side, much traditional Roman Catholic theology has firmly asserted that there is only one Church, that the Roman Catholic Church is that Church, and that outside of it there is no guaranteed salvation.

Echoes of these loud voices from the past are still heard, but they are now largely replaced by less hostile and even welcoming voices and attitudes. Instead of 'papists', members of the Roman Church are now described as 'Roman Catholics'; and Protestants are now 'separated brethren' rather than heretics or schismatics. It seems that everywhere Protestants meet officially, there are Roman Catholic observers; just as, at the opening of the Second Vatican Council, Protestant observers sat opposite the cardinals in St. Peter's Church in Rome. There is no single reason why attitudes have changed. However, the ecumenical movement which began at Edinburgh in 1910 has played a large part, and we shall now consider the new Roman Catholic attitude, as it is expressed in the *Decree on Ecumenism* published by the Pope from the Second Vatican Council, on 21 November 1964.

The problem for Roman Catholics

The way in which Roman Catholicism had expressed its view of what the Church of God was, made it difficult for her theologians and bishops to adopt a positive attitude towards the Protestant Churches and denominations. It was much easier for them to relate positively to the Eastern Orthodox Church, for example. Their answer was not to alter the doctrine of the Church, but to look for new ways of expressing all or part of the doctrine so that a place for Protestant Christianity could be found.

Traditional Roman Catholic teaching about the Church establishes two basic principles, which are repeated in the *Dogmatic Constitution on the Church* (the *Lumen Gentium*) which Vatican II produced. Firstly, full visible unity of the Church on earth is seen as being necessary and required by the will of God. Visible unity is part of the true being *(esse)* of the Church, not part of its well-being *(bene esse)*. The second principle is intimately related to the first. Visible unity exists: it is created around the college and order of bishops, and the bishop of Rome is its centre and head. Every bishop in his diocese is a sign of unity of the Church, and the Pope in Rome is the sign of its universal unity.

And so on the one hand, the members of the Second Vatican Council were committed to these principles, and at the same time they genuinely wanted to affirm that Protestants were true Christians, loved by God the Father, redeemed by God the Son and being sanctified by God the Spirit. They set out accordingly to find, while still retaining their principles, a way of affirming that the 'separated brethren' were truly in union with our Lord Jesus Christ.

The problem can be stated as two questions. Firstly — what is the position of the individual Protestant, considered as a sincere believer in our Lord Jesus Christ? And, secondly, what of the congregations, national Churches and denominations (associations of congregations), considered as groups of sincere believers in our Lord Jesus Christ? Significantly, the *Decree* recognises that the blame for the divisions in Christendom in the sixteenth century cannot belong to Protestantism alone. Both sides were to blame. The *Decree* deals with these two questions in the light of that fact.

Concerning individual members of Protestant communities as they now exist, the *Decree* has this to say: 'One cannot impute the sin of separation to those who at present are born into these Communities and are instilled therein with Christ's faith.' It continues: 'the Catholic Church accepts them with respect and affection as brothers.' Why? Because, the *Decree* affirms, 'men who believe in Christ and have been properly baptised are brought into certain, though imperfect, communion with the Catholic Church.' (We will return to this concept of 'imperfect communion' later.) 'All those justified by faith through baptism are incorporated into Christ. They therefore have a right to be honoured by the title of Christian, and are properly regarded as brothers in the Lord by the sons of the Catholic Church.'

In passing from the answer to the first question to the answer to the second, the *Decree* reads:

> Moreover some, even very many, of the most significant elements or endowments which together go to build up and give life to the Church herself can exist outside the boundaries of the Catholic Church: the written word of God; the life of grace; faith, hope and charity, along with other interior gifts of the Holy Spirit and visible elements. All of these, which come from Christ and lead back to him, belong by right to the one Church of Christ.

> The brethren divided from us also carry out many of the sacred actions of the Christian religion. Undoubtedly, in ways that vary according to the conditions of each Church or Community, these actions can truly engender a life of grace and can rightly be described as capable of providing access to the community of salvation.

To Protestants, these sentences appear to be a common-sense recognition of the fact which they well know; that there is a genuine Christianity within their Churches.

In the light of what has been stated already, the *Decree* makes a remarkable statement in facing the second question:

> It follows that these separated Churches and Communities, though we believe they suffer from defects already mentioned, have by no means been deprived of significance and importance in the mystery of salvation. For the Spirit of Christ has not refrained from using them as the means of salvation which derive their efficacy from the very fullness of grace and truth entrusted to the Catholic Church.

This represents the most positive, official declaration ever made by the Church of Rome concerning non-Roman Catholic communities.

However, the traditional teaching is not forgotten. The next paragraph reads:

> Nevertheless, our separated brethren, whether considered as individuals or as Communities and Churches, are not blessed with that unity which Jesus Christ wished to bestow on all those whom he has regenerated and vivified into one body and newness of life — that unity which the Holy Scriptures and the revered tradition of the Church proclaim. For it is through Christ's Catholic Church alone, which is the all-embracing means of salvation, that the fullness of the means of salvation can be obtained. It was to the apostolic college alone, of which Peter is the head, that we believe our Lord entrusted all the blessings of the New Covenant, in order to establish on earth the one Body of Christ into which all those should be fully incorporated who already belong in any way to God's People. During its pilgrimage on earth, this People, though still in its members liable to sin, is growing in Christ and is being gently guided by God, according to his hidden designs, until it happily arrives at the fullness of eternal glory in the heavenly Jerusalem.

What this paragraph certainly says is that, while Protestant communities enjoy many divine blessings, they lack the fullness of communion (or 'perfect communion') with Christ and his whole Church.

We have already seen the distinction made between members of Protestant Churches, who are said to be in a 'certain though imperfect communion' with Christ and his Church, and members of the Roman Catholic Church who are said to be in a 'perfect communion'. The difference appears to be this. In the Roman Church, it is argued, there exists the valid ordained ministry of bishops and priests, and also the full sacramental life as expressed in the celebration of the Eucharist and the six other sacraments. This Church is united historically (through space and time) with Christ and the first apostles. It is also united with Christ now, by the Spirit who proceeds from Christ, bringing grace and gifts. It is a visible unity, ruled by its bishops (with the Pope as their head) under Christ the Lord who moment by moment gives salvation to his pilgrim people.

By contrast, it is pointed out, while Protestant Christians enjoy the immediate experience of the Spirit's presence and work and know the salvation given by Christ the Lord, they do not have the dimension of the historical, continuing reality of the Church led and ruled by the college of bishops. Their experience of God in Christ and of the richness he has given to the Catholic Church is restricted by their separation from the authentic historical, continuing, visible Church of God. They certainly have grace — but they could have more. They certainly have truth — but they could have more. Their communion with Christ and his Church is, as a result, certain but imperfect.

The Roman Catholic approach to other Christians

Believing as they do that their Church is divinely

34

approved, Roman Catholics might perhaps enter into fraternal relationships with separated brethren in an arrogant, triumphalist manner. But the *Decree*, and several official documents that followed it, demands and commends a humble and positive attitude. 'There can be no ecumenism worthy of the name without a change of heart,' it urges, 'for it is from newness of attitudes, from self-denial and unstinted love, that yearnings for unity take their rise and grow towards maturity. We should pray, therefore, to the divine Spirit for the grace to be genuinely self-denying, humble, gentle in the service of others, and to have an attitude of brotherly generosity toward them.'

Prayer is to continue for the unity of the Church; where this includes worshipping with separated brethren, the local bishops are to decide what is acceptable and practicable. There is to be a genuine attempt to understand the Protestant outlook, including not only its theologies but also its history, spiritual and liturgical life, religious psychology and cultural background. And furthermore, in theological education, the various parts of the curriculum are to be taught in such a way that not just Roman Catholic but also Protestant views and insights are conveyed. Where the Roman Catholic position is being explained to Protestants, great care is to be taken to present it in its purity and integrity. However, this does not mean that there is only one philosophical or cultural way of expressing it; the essence of the Roman Catholic position can be expressed in a variety of forms. The *Decree* adds that though all Roman Catholic dogma is important, 'there exists an order of hierarchy of truths' — some things are primary and must be presented before any others.

Regarding the differences between Roman Catholicism and Protestantism, a number of different issues are taken up in the section entitled 'The separated Churches and ecclesiastical Communities in the West'. 'There are very weighty differences not only of a historical, sociological, psychological and cultural nature,' it points out, 'but especially in the interpretation of revealed truth.' Weighty differences are also found in the teaching on 'the mystery and ministry of the Church and the role of Mary in the work of salvation'. On the importance of the Scriptures, there is agreement; but regarding their relationship to the Church, there are major differences of belief. According to Catholic belief, there is an authentic teaching office in the Church which has a special role in the explanation of and proclamation of the written word of God. Finally, because the separated brethren do not possess the sacrament of orders (bishops and priests in the apostolic succession), they cannot have the fullness of sacramental life in their communities.

It is important to acknowledge differences, but things that are good should be commended; and so the *Decree* ends with this statement regarding Protestants:

> The Christian way of life of these brethren is nourished by faith in Christ. It is strengthened by the grace of baptism and the hearing of God's Word. This way of life expresses itself in private prayer, in meditation on the Bible, in Christian family life, and in services of worship offered by Communities assembled to praise God. Furthermore, their worship sometimes displays notable features of an ancient, common liturgy.
>
> The faith by which they believe in Christ bears fruit in praise and thanksgiving for the benefits received from the hands of God. Joined to it are a lively sense of justice and a true neighbourly charity. This active faith has produced many organisations for the relief of spiritual and bodily distress, the education of youth, the advancement of human social conditions, and the promotion of peace throughout the world.
>
> And if in moral matters there are many Christians who do not always understand the gospel in the same way as Catholics, and do not admit the same solutions

for the more difficult problems of modern society, nevertheless they share our desire to obey the apostolic command: 'Whatever you do in word or in work, do all in the name of the Lord Jesus, giving thanks to God the Father through him' (Col.3:17). Hence, the ecumenical dialogue could start with discussions concerning the application of the gospel to moral questions.

There have been mixed Roman Catholic and Protestant discussion groups in many places in Europe and America studying contemporary moral issues. Also, many members of both sides — particularly young people — have been jointly involved in work on behalf of the needy in God's world. Official theological commissions from several Protestant bodies have met with official Roman Catholic commissions for dialogue and discussion — in the USA this has been done both by the Methodists and the Lutherans, and their reports make interesting reading. At an international level, the Anglican Communion of Churches has arranged talks between its theological commission and an official Roman Catholic commission; and their unanimous reports have caused considerable discussion, especially the final one concerning the place of the Pope in a reunited Christendom. No doubt these forms of official dialogue will continue and increase.

As more and more priests and clergy are trained together, or at least share a part of their training in common, understanding between Roman Catholics and Protestants will grow. In the same way, understanding will be increased and encouraged as collaboration takes place over matters concerning the dignity of the human person. In campaigns on behalf of unborn children or against racial discrimination — to name only two contemporary issues — Roman Catholics and Protestants often walk hand in hand.

But there is still hesitation, especially on the part of the hierarchy in the Roman Church, over joining together in the Lord's Supper (the Eucharist). Roman Catholics are usually advised not to receive the holy elements at a Protestant service; and while Protestants are encouraged to attend Mass, they do not normally receive the holy elements from the hands of the Roman priest. This attitude appears uncharitable, but the real reason lies in a profound theology of the Eucharist, or Mass. By its very nature it signifies visible unity — 'We are all one.' It is given by God to express and strengthen an existing unity. And so until there is genuine visible unity, it is wrong for those who are separated to participate in the same Eucharist.

Why then is there no visible unity? Because certain major differences separate Protestants and Roman Catholics. We will consider some of these in the next chapter.

4: On what foundation?

There was never a time in the history of the western Church during the 'Dark' or 'Middle' Ages when the Scriptures were officially demoted. On the contrary, they were considered infallible and inerrant, and were held in the highest honour. However, within this Church, which claimed to treasure and preserve the Bible, there grew up a complex assortment of 'traditions' which in practice effectively denied the message of the Bible in certain respects. These 'traditions' found expression in ecclesiastical rules and accepted practices. There were in addition liturgies, or services of worship, and a great body of teaching; some of this was official (called 'dogma'), and some semi-official (called 'doctrine'). Consequently the Bible was usually interpreted within the Church by the bishops and theologians so as to buttress the traditions, liturgies and teaching. There were exceptions — men such as John Wycliffe and John Huss, who called for reform.

Early Protestant statements

Between 1515 and 1530, certain members of the great Church began to read the Scriptures — especially the New Testament — with searching and penetrating eyes. They were able to do this because of the new learning and methods of the Renaissance. As they read, they began to realise that many aspects of the life, worship and teaching of the Church appeared to be contrary to the standards set by Jesus and his apostles. One person who felt this keenly was Martin Luther, whose concern over the practice of selling Indulgences (official remission of punishment for sin) led to his nailing of the ninety-five theses to the church door in Wittenberg, on 31 October 1517. This action can be said to have set the Reformation in motion.

In 1523, Huldreich Zwingli initiated the Protestant Reformation in Switzerland with his *Sixty-seven Articles*, which were debated in Zurich. These are more comprehensive then the ninety-five theses of Luther. The claim that each of them carries is that they are Scripture-based and in accordance with Scripture. Here are two of them:

Article X. Just as a man is demented whose members operate without his head, lacerating, wounding and harming himself, so also are the members of Christ demented when they undertake something without Christ, their Head, tormenting and burdening themselves with foolish ordinances.

Article XI. Therefore we perceive that the so-called clerical traditions with their pomp, riches, hierarchy, titles and laws are a cause of all nonsense, because they are not in agreement with Christ, the Head.

Here the claim is that Christ can only be known through the authoritative Scriptures; to listen to Christ clearly involves listening to the pure message of the Bible.

Five years later, the city of Berne expressed the principles of its new Protestantism in the *Ten Theses* (1528). The first two are as follows:

1. The holy, Christian Church, whose only Head is Christ, is born of the Word of God, abides in the same, and does not listen to the voice of a stranger.

2. The Church of Christ makes no laws or commandments without God's Word. Hence all human traditions, which are called ecclesiastical commandments, are binding only in so far as they are based on and commanded by God's Word.

Here again Christ and the Bible are closely identified

with each other. And the meaning of these principles in one area of the Church's life is explained in the seventh thesis:

> 7. Scripture knows nothing of a purgatory after this life. Hence all offices for the dead such as vigils, masses, requiems, devotions, repeated after the seventh or thirtieth day of each year, lamps, candles and such like are in vain.

The *Theses* end, 'May all things be to the honour of God and his holy Word!'

The same condemnation of human traditions which do not 'belong solely to the maintenance of peace, honesty and good order in the assembly of Christians' is found in the *Tetrapolitan Confession* (1530) and the *Geneva Confession* (1536). The latter (section 17) declares that 'all laws and regulations made binding on conscience which oblige the faithful to things not commanded by God, or establish another service of God than that which he demands . . . we condemn as perverse doctrines of Satan . . . . It is in this estimation that we hold pilgrimages, monasteries, distinctions of food, prohibition of marriage, confessions and other things.'

It is one thing to affirm the priority of Scripture and its judgement upon the traditions of the Church, but it is another thing to decide how the Bible is to be interpreted. This is how the *First Helvetic Confession* (1536) dealt with the matter:

> 1. *Concerning Holy Scripture* The holy, divine, Biblical Scripture, which is the Word of God inspired by the Holy Spirit and delivered to the world by the prophets and apostles, is the most ancient, most perfect and loftiest teaching and alone deals with everything that serves the true knowledge, love and honour of God, as well as true piety and the making of a godly, honest and blessed life.

2. Concerning the Interpretation of Scripture This holy, divine Scripture is to be interpreted in no other way than out of itself and is to be explained by the rule of faith and love.

3. Concerning the Early Teachers Where the holy fathers and early teachers, who have explained and expounded the Scripture, have not departed from this rule, we want to recognise and consider them not only as expositors of Scripture, but as elect instruments through whom God has spoken and operated.

4. Concerning Doctrines of Men We regard all other human doctrines and articles which lead us away from God and true faith as vain and ineffectual, no matter how attractive, fine, esteemed and of long usage they may be, as Saint Matthew himself attests in chapter 15 where he says: 'In vain do they worship me, teaching as doctrines the precepts of men.'

5. The Purpose of Holy Scripture and That to Which it Finally Points The entire biblical Scripture is solely concerned that man understands that God is kind and gracious to him and that He has publicly exhibited and demonstrated this His kindness to the whole human race through Christ His Son. However, it comes to us and is received by faith alone, and is manifested and demonstrated by love for our neighbour.

The basic principles of the Reformed Faith are contained in these statements of the *Confession* — principles which were later to be elaborated in lengthier confessions.

Meanwhile, within German Lutheranism, the *Augsburg Confession* (1530) had appeared. The last of its twenty-two articles summarised its explanation of important aspects of the Christian faith as the German Protestants understood it, claiming that:

. . . there is nothing which is discrepant with the Scriptures, or with the Church Catholic, or even with the Roman Church, so far as that Church is known from writers (the writings of the Fathers). This being the case, they judge us harshly who insist that we shall be regarded as heretics. But the dissension is concerning certain traditions and abuses, which without authority have crept into the churches . . .'

Here an attempt is being made to separate unacceptable traditions and abuses from the Church as it was in the early centuries and to see these as having grown up later. Of course it is true that the Lutherans were much more ready — as were the Anglicans — to accept old, ecclesiastical traditions in the Church so long as they did not obviously contradict basic teaching of Scripture.

Part II of the *Augsburg Confession* lists abuses of the late Mediaeval Church, now, in Lutheran Germany, corrected. Holy Communion is now in two kinds (the bread and the wine); priests may marry; the Mass has been reformed; spoken confession has been put on a proper basis; food regulations have been abandoned; monastic vows have been cancelled, and the excessive powers of bishops curtailed. The Confession claims that all this has been done in the light of the Word of God.

The Council of Trent

On 8 April 1546, the Roman Catholic answer to the Protestant insistence on 'Sola scriptura' (Scripture alone) came with the issuing of two decrees; the major one was 'Concerning the Canonical Scriptures', and the subsiduary one, 'Concerning the edition and the use of the Sacred Books'.

The first decree states that the truth and discipline of the gospel of Christ is contained in written books and unwritten traditions, the contents of which can be traced back to the Lord Jesus himself or to one or other of his apostles. In the light of this, the Council 'following the example of the orthodox Fathers, receives and venerates with an equal affection of piety and reverence all the books both of the Old and the New Testament . . . as also the said traditions, as well as those appertaining to faith as to morals, as having been dictated, either by Christ's own word of mouth, or by the Holy Ghost, and preserved in the Catholic Church by a continuous succession'. The important expression to note here is: ' . . . receives and venerates with an equal affection of piety and reverence' the written books (the Holy Scriptures) and the unwritten traditions (which the decree does not list).

The first decree did list the books of Scripture. The Protestants had been demanding that the Hebrew canon of the Old Testament should be accepted; the tradition of the Church for centuries had been to accept in addition the books, originally written by the Jews in Greek, known as the Apocrypha. The decree listed the books as found in the *Vulgate Bible*, which is the Latin translation of the Hebrew canon plus the apocryphal books.

The Vulgate is named in the second decree, and announced as the definitive Latin translation of the Bible. Furthermore, it was decreed that this Bible should only be interpreted according to the sense which 'Holy mother Church . . . hath held and doth hold'. The Vulgate was the official Bible version used in the First and Second Vatican Councils.

The most common Roman Catholic interpretation of the first decree was that divine revelation is divided into two types. Some revelation is contained only in oral traditions; other revelation, it was stated, is contained only in the sacred Scriptures. This was a very convenient division; critics pointing out that certain doctrines or ceremonies were not to be found in the Bible could be told that this was indeed true, for their basis was in the oral tradition.

There has been considerable debate in the present century between Roman Catholics as to the precise relationship between Scripture and Tradition (or traditions), as will be seen when we look at the teaching of the Second Vatican Council.

Later Protestant Statements

Various leading reformers wrote books defending Protestant principles against the decrees of the Council of Trent; the two most famous and learned were that written by John Calvin for the Reformed Churches, and that by Martin Chemnitz for the Lutheran Churches. Also, Protestants formulating confessions of faith after the Council had met took its teachings into account, as will be seen as we look at various *Confessions* dating from 1559.

The French Confession of Faith (1559) described God as revealing himself in his creation, and, more clearly, in his Word originally given in oracles and then written down in the books of Holy Scripture. In Article III the biblical books are listed. The list follows the Hebrew canon of the Old Testament, implicitly rejecting the Apocrypha. The Confession continues:

IV. We know these books to be canonical, and the sure rule of our faith, not so much by the common accord and consent of the Church, as by the testimony and inward illumination of the Holy Spirit, which enables us to distinguish them from other ecclesiastical books upon which, however useful, we can not found any articles of faith.

V. We believe that the Word contained in these books has proceeded from God, and receives its authority from him alone, and not from men. And inasmuch as it is the rule of all truth, containing all that is necessary for the service of God and for our salvation, it is not lawful for men, nor even for angels, to add to it, to take away from it, or to change it. Whence it follows that no authority whether of antiquity, or custom, or numbers, or human wisdom, or judgments, or proclamations, or edicts, or decrees, or councils, or visions, or miracles, should be opposed to these Holy Scriptures, but, on the contrary all things should be examined, regulated, and reformed according to them. And therefore we confess the three creeds, to wit: the Apostles', the Nicene, and the Athanasian, because they are in accordance with the Word of God.

The Holy Spirit is the author of Scripture; and as we read, we know that Scripture is God's Word because the Holy Spirit witnesses to our heart that this is so. This basic teaching is much emphasised by John Calvin (*Institutes*, 1:7:4; 3:1:1; 3:1:3; 3:2:15, 33–36). It is also found in other Reformed confessions of the period. Also, there was agreement between Anglicans, Lutherans and Reformed that the ancient creeds were acceptable because they were in accordance with the Word of God.

The *Belgic Confession* of 1561 lists the sixty-six books of the Hebrew Old Testament and Greek New Testament canons. Following Calvin, it explains that the basis of accepting them as from God is not that the Church as such approves them, but more particularly because the Holy Spirit 'witnesseth in our hearts that they are from God, whereof they carry the evidence in themselves'. It goes on to explain the Protestant attitude to the extra books contained in the Vulgate:

VI. The Difference Between the Canonical and Apocryphal Books We distinguish these sacred books from the apocryphal, viz., the third and fourth book of Esdras, the books of Tobias, Judith, Wisdom, Jesus Syrach, Baruch, the appendix to the book of Esther, the Song of the Three Children in the Furnace, the History of Susannah, of Bel and the Dragon, the Prayer of Manasses, and the two books of Maccabees. All which the Church may read and take instruction from, so far as they agree with the canonical books; but they are far from having such power and efficacy as that we may from their testimony confirm any point of faith or of the Christian religion; much less to detract from the authority of the other sacred books.

There is a similar statement in Article VI of the *Thirty-Nine Articles* (1562) of the Church of England. Since the sixteenth century, these books have been read once a year as part of the daily lectionary of the Church. But the Protestants made the important point that Judaism never approved the books of the Apocrypha as authoritative Scripture. So, as the Church receives the Old Testament canon from the Jews, it ought to receive the authentic Hebrew canon. (Having said which, it should nevertheless be realised that the apocryphal books were accepted from early times, by both Eastern and Western branches of the Church, as true Holy Scripture.)

The Protestant attitude to the so-called 'General', or 'Ecumenical' Church Councils is recorded in several Confessions. Article XXI of the *Thirty-Nine Articles* reflects the close identification of Church with State in the sixteenth century:

> General Councils may not be gathered together without the commandment and will of Princes. And when they be gathered together (forasmuch as they be an assembly of men, whereof all be not governed with the Spirit and the Word of God) they may err, and sometimes have erred, even in things pertaining unto God. Wherefore things ordained by them as necessary to salvation have neither strength nor authority, unless it may be declared that they be taken out of Holy Scripture.

The *Scots Confession* declares (Chapter XX):

> As we do not rashly condemn what good men, assembled together in General Councils lawfully gathered, have set before us; so we do not receive uncritically whatever has been declared to men under

the name of the General Councils, for it is plain that, being human, some of them have manifestly erred, and that in matters of great weight and importance. So far then as the Council confirms its decrees by the plain Word of God, so far do we reverence and embrace them. But if men, under the name of a Council, pretend to forge for us new articles of faith, or to make decisions contrary to the Word of God, then we must utterly deny them as the doctrines of devils, drawing our souls from the voice of the one God to follow the doctrines and teachings of men.

Everything must be tested against the written Word of God: and the written Word has to be interpreted.

The *Second Helvetic Confession* (1566) deals in its second chapter with: the task of interpreting the Holy Scriptures; of receiving the interpretations of the Greek and Latin Fathers of the first six or seven centuries; of the authority of the decrees of councils; and, finally, of human or ecclesiastical traditions. It has this to say concerning the interpretation of Scripture:

> We hold that interpretation of the Scripture to be orthodox and genuine which is gleaned from the Scriptures themselves (from the nature of the language in which they were written, likewise according to the circumstances in which they were set down, and expounded in the light of like and unlike passages and of many and clearer passages) and which agree with the rule of faith and love, and contributes much to the glory of God and man's salvation.

This is the classic Protestant approach. A part of Scripture which is difficult should be understood in the light of other, clearer parts — a principle set out in more detail in the official Church of England homily 'A fruitful exhortation to the reading of Holy Scripture' (*Book of Homilies*, homily 1).

Addressing the Council of Trent's claim that certain

traditions of the Church could be traced back to oral instruction from the first apostles, this *Swiss Confession* explains:

> *Traditions of Men* Likewise we reject human traditions, even if they be adorned with high-sounding titles, as though they were divine and apostolical, delivered to the Church by the living voice of the apostles, and, as it were, through the hands of apostolical men to succeeding bishops which, when compared with the Scriptures, disagree with them; and by their disagreement show that they are not apostolic at all. For as the apostles did not contradict themselves in doctrine, so the apostolic men did not set forth things contrary to the apostles. On the contrary, it would be wicked to assert that the apostles by a living voice delivered anything contrary to their writings. Paul affirms expressly that he taught the same things in all churches (1 Cor. 4:17). And, again 'For we write you nothing but what you can read and understand' (2 Cor. 1:13). Also, in another place, he testifies that he and his disciples — that is, apostolic men — walked in the same way, and jointly by the same Spirit did all things (2 Cor. 12:18). Moreover, the Jews in former times had the traditions of their elders; but these traditions were severely rejected by the Lord, indicating that the keeping of them hinders God's law and that God is worshipped in vain by such traditions (Matt. 15:1ff.; Mark 7:1 ff).

Here again, we encounter the fundamental difference of approach between the Protestant and Roman Catholic mind of the sixteenth century.

Of course it is possible that when they condemned traditions, the Protestants had in mind the worst (in their view) practices and abuses; and that the Roman Catholics felt that as all traditions seemed to be under attack they had better defend all of them.

In practice, the Protestants differed among themselves

concerning the exact amount of mediaeval ecclesiastical practice, ritual and ceremonial they were prepared to allow into their respective Churches. It is generally true to say that the Lutherans and Anglicans had a more positive attitude to certain traditions, ritual and ceremonial than the Reformed Churches (and later the Baptist and Free Churches) had. Their position was expressed in the Greek word, *adiaphora* — 'things indifferent', neither commanded nor forbidden by God. Anglicans and Lutherans thereby retained the rite of confirmation, used certain mediaeval clerical vestments, and worshipped with the help of liturgies which were recognisably adapted from mediaeval services. The Reformed Churches, on the other hand, took as a basic principle that everything in doctrine and practice must be proved out of the Word of God; and so they rejected some things which Anglicans and Lutherans were happy to use.

The mature, or developed, Reformed position on Scripture — its canon, inspiration and interpretation — is to be found in chapter 1 of the *Westminster Confession of Faith* (1647) and also in chapter 1 of the *Savoy Declaration of Faith and Order* (1658). The latter is essentially the same text as the former, with only a few minor changes. Also, much the same teaching is found in chapter 1 of the *Confession of Faith* (1677) of the English (Calvinistic) Baptists, which was incorporated in the 1742 *Philadelphia Baptist Confession* in America.

This would be an appropriate point at which to summarise the Protestant position on Scripture and Tradition.

God has revealed his mind and will to prophets and apostles, and he has revealed himself in Jesus of Nazareth. The sixty-six books of the Holy Scriptures, originally written in Greek and Hebrew, are the authentic record of this divine revelation produced under the guidance of the Holy Spirit. So, living under the Lordship of Christ, the Church is to base its doctrines, morals and worship on the written Word of God.

Nothing which contradicts the written Word is to be accepted in the Church; certain things may be allowed, which are judged to be in accordance with its general spirit. Ancient Catholic doctrines are to be accepted primarily because they are in agreement with the Word of God. All teaching of councils, synods and bishops must be scrutinised to see whether or not it is in harmony with the Word of God. Tradition can never be venerated with the same affection as the Holy Scriptures, for the simple reason that tradition is not divinely guaranteed and is therefore fallible and subject to error.

Roman Catholics and Protestants do not disagree at all as to whether or not the Bible is the inspired, authoritative Word of God. Both affirm that the Bible was produced under special conditions so as to be free from error and thus to be the infallible guide of the Church. They do differ as to the extent of the canon of Scripture and as to its relationship to tradition. As we turn to the teaching of the Second Vatican Council we shall find that the Roman Catholic position, though expressed very attractively, remains fundamentally unchanged.

The Second Vatican Council

The *Dogmatic Constitution on Divine Revelation* had a long history before it was accepted by the Council and set forth by the Pope on 18 November 1965. It was much revised and much debated. The final version was seen not merely as a theological document, but also as a proclamation of good news to the world.

It begins with a very attractive description of God's self-revelation to the world, primarily in Jesus Christ the Incarnate Son. The second chapter, 'The transmission of divine revelation', is so important for our discussion that we need to consider it carefully and quote it in full.

The first paragraph (paragraph 7 of the Constitution) describes one source of divine revelation, expressed in two methods of transmission. The source of revelation for the Church and the world is Christ the Lord in a primary sense, and also in a secondary sense the apostles. The two forms in which this revelation is passed on are in writing (the Bible) and by the spoken word (tradition).

> In his gracious goodness, God has seen to it that what he had revealed for the salvation of all nations would abide perpetually in its full integrity and be handed on to all generations. Therefore Christ the Lord in whom the full revelation of the supreme God is brought to completion (see 1 Cor. 1:20; 3:13; 4:6), commissioned the apostles to preach to all men that gospel which is the source of all saving truth and moral teaching, and to impart to them heavenly gifts. This gospel had been promised in former times through the prophets, and Christ himself had fulfilled it and promulgated it with his lips. This commission was faithfully fulfilled by the apostles who by their oral preaching, by example, and by observances handed on what they had received from the lips of Christ, from living with him, and from what he did, or what they had learned through the prompting of the Holy Spirit. The commission was fulfilled, too, by those apostles and apostolic men who under the inspiration of the same Holy Spirit committed the message of salvation to writing.
>
> But in order to keep the gospel for ever whole and alive within the Church, the apostles left bishops as their successors, 'handing over' to them 'the authority to teach in their own place'. This sacred tradition, therefore, and sacred scripture of both the old and the new testament are like a mirror in which the pilgrim Church on earth looks at God, from whom she has received everything, until she is brought finally to see him as he is, face to face (see 1 John 3:2).

Most Roman Catholic theologians regard this way of putting the matter as superior to the common idea within their Church since the sixteenth century, that there are two sources of revelation — Scripture and tradition. Paragraph 8 explains how the transmission of revelation within the Church led to the production and acceptance of those books called the New Testament; and how it also led to oral tradition existing alongside those books, expressed both in an understanding of the meaning of revelation and in the expression of this meaning in the life, witness and worship of the Church under the guidance of the episcopate.

And so the apostolic preaching, which is expressed in a special way in the inspired books, was to be preserved by an unending succession of preachers until the end of time. Therefore the apostles, handing on what they themselves had received, warn the faithful to hold fast to the traditions which they have learned either by word of mouth or by letter (see 2 Thess. 2:15), and to fight in defence of the faith handed on once and for all (see Jud. 3). Now what was handed on by the apostles includes everything which contributes toward the holiness of life and increase in faith of the People of God; and so the Church, in her teaching, life and worship, perpetuates and hands on to all generations all that she herself is, all that she believes.

This tradition which comes from the Apostles develops in the Church with the help of the Holy Spirit. For there is a growth in the understanding of the realities and the words which have been handed down. This happens through the contemplation and study made by believers, who treasure these things in their hearts (see Luke 2:19,51), through a penetrating understanding of the spiritual realities which they experience, and through the preaching of those who have received through episcopal succession the sure gift of truth. For as the centuries succeed one another, the Church constantly moves forward toward the fullness of divine truth until the words of God reach their complete fulfilment in her.

The words of the holy Fathers witness to the presence of this living tradition, whose wealth is poured into the practice and life of the believing and

praying Church. Through the same tradition the
Church's full canon of the sacred books is known and
the sacred writings themselves are more profoundly
understood and unceasingly made active in her; and
thus God, who spoke of old, uninterruptedly converses
with the bride of his beloved Son; and the Holy Spirit,
through whom the living voice of the gospel resounds
in the Church, and through her, in the world, leads
unto all truth those who believe and make the word of
Christ dwell abundantly in them (see Col. 3:16).

The reference to the 'holy Fathers' is to the orthodox
Christian writers of East and West, of the first six or
seven centuries.

Finally in paragraphs 9 and 10 we encounter the
declaration that equal veneration is to be given to sacred
tradition and sacred Scripture, and that the Church, in
which the tradition exists, has a duty of interpreting the
Scriptures.

Hence there exists a close connection and communica-
tion between sacred tradition and sacred scripture. For
both of them, flowing from the same divine well-
spring, in a certain way merge into a unity and tend
toward the same end. For sacred scripture is the word
of God inasmuch as it is consigned to writing under the
inspiration of the divine Spirit, while sacred tradition
takes the Word of God, entrusted by Christ the Lord
and the Holy Spirit to the apostles, and hands it on to
their successors, in its full purity, so that led by the
light of the Spirit of truth, they may in proclaiming it
preserve this Word of God faithfully, explain it, and
make it more widely known. Consequently it is not
from sacred scripture alone that the Church draws her
certainty about everything which has been revealed.
Therefore both sacred tradition and sacred scripture
are to be accepted and venerated with the same sense
of loyalty and reverence.

Sacred tradition and sacred scripture form one

sacred deposit of the word of God, committed to the Church. Holding fast to this deposit the entire holy people united with their shepherds remain always steadfast in the teaching of the apostles, in the common life, in the breaking of the bread and in prayers, (see Acts 2, 42, Greek text), so that holding to, practising and professing the heritage of the faith, it becomes on the part of the bishops and faithful a single common effort.

But the task of authentically interpreting the word of God, whether written or handed on, has been entrusted exclusively to the living teaching office of the Church, whose authority is exercised in the name of Jesus Christ. This teaching office is not above the word of God, but serves it, teaching only what has been handed on, listening to it devoutly, guarding it scrupulously and explaining it faithfully in accord with a divine commission and with the help of the Holy Spirit; it draws from this one deposit of faith everything which it presents for belief as divinely revealed.

It is clear, therefore, that sacred tradition, sacred scripture and the teaching authority of the Church, in accord with God's most wise design, are so linked and joined together that one cannot stand without the others, and that all together and each in its own way under the action of the one Holy Spirit contribute effectively to the salvation of souls.

Though it is nowhere stated, it is reasonable to assume that the two famous dogmas concerning Mary the mother of Jesus arose from the oral tradition of the Church. The Immaculate Conception and the Bodily Assumption of the Blessed Virgin Mary (at which we shall look later) are dogmas which, while not being taught in the Bible, are not actually denied by it. Since they did not arise out of the text of the Bible, and since it is claimed that they are based on divine revelation, then they must have been (on the argument of Vatican II) implicit within the oral tradition from the beginning. The existence of these dogmas, and the claims for tradition expressed in this *Dogmatic Constitution*, contrast with the basic Protestant claim that all doctrine necessary for salvation must be clearly based on the Bible.

In further chapters of the Constitution there is much teaching that biblical Protestants can gladly accept (in chapter 6 there is the command: 'Easy access to sacred Scripture should be provided for all the Christian faithful'). However, the teaching that revelation has one source and two forms of transmission remains opposed to the continuing Protestant position, that revelation has one source and only one guaranteed form of transmission. For Protestants, tradition — however authentic — must be subject to the written Word of God, rightly interpreted. Though there have been many conferences, commissions, committees and individual theologians within Protestantism which have addressed themselves to the relationship of Scripture and tradition, there has been no authoritative statement from any of the major Protestant Churches or denominations which changes the fundamental position adopted in the confessions of faith quoted earlier in this chapter.

5: By whose authority?

In the earliest days of the Church the primary confession of faith was 'Jesus is Lord', or, 'Jesus, the Christ, is Lord.'

After rising from the dead, Jesus declared: 'All authority in heaven and earth has been given to me. Go therefore and make disciples of all nations, baptising them in the name of the Father and of the Son and of the Holy Spirit, teaching them to observe all that I have commanded you; and lo, I am with you always, to the close of the age' (Matthew 28:18–20).

When he had ascended into heaven, exalted as King of kings and Lord of lords, Jesus was in a position to fulfil his promises to the apostles and the disciples (John 14–16). From the Father he sent them the Holy Spirit (Acts 2), whose task was to create the community of the Church and to give its members gifts for the exercise of ministry and oversight. 'And his gifts were that some should be apostles, some prophets, some evangelists, some pastors and teachers, to equip the saints for ministry, for building up the Body of Christ . . .' (Ephesians 4:11–12). So the Church — to quote St Paul again — is the 'household of God', being 'built upon the foundation of the apostles and prophets, Christ himself being the cornerstone' (Ephesians 2:20).

These are foundational truths which are accepted unquestioningly both by Roman Catholics and by Protestants. Both sides also agree wholeheartedly that the authoritative message of the apostles and prophets was written down in various ways (the Gospels and the Letters) to form the collection of books we call the New Testament. It is well known that there has been a continuing debate over which came first — the Church or the Scriptures. What happened was that the apostles, making use of the Old Testament which they received as God's Word, preached the gospel they had learned from Jesus as the Holy Spirit illuminated their minds. They also wrote down their understanding of the gospel of Christ, for the churches' use. After they died, what remained was the memory of what they had taught, and the words they had written down. Some of the latter material was collected together, and was accepted by the Church as sacred, the 'New Testament'.

In one sense, therefore, the Church came first; for it actually decided which books to include and which to exclude from the canon of the New Testament. However, in another sense, the message written down in those books was the very message which, in the power of the Spirit, had created the Church. Thus, the Church only recognised what in fact had brought it into being and maintained it in existence.

The central point is that both sides accept the authority of the Scriptures, and both believe that Christ the Lord through the Holy Spirit uses their contents as his authoritative word to the Church and to the world.

Protestant and Roman Catholic historians may well agree as to the way in which what might be termed 'external authority' was developed and used in the Church as it evolved as an institution, over the next fifteen centuries. Where disagreement arises is in the theological evaluation of that authority. Could such 'external authorities' really be claimed to be the result of Christ's guidance of the Church and his rule over it by the Holy Spirit?

That the chief officers of the Church became known as bishop, priest and deacon; that certain bishoprics, for example those at Alexandria, Antioch, Constantinople, Jerusalem and Rome, were regarded as exercising authority over others in their areas; and that in the western part of the Roman Empire the Bishop of Rome came to wield great power and be regarded as the successor of St Peter and the vicar of Christ — these are well known facts. Furthermore, everybody accepts that there were seven international assemblies of bishops known as ecumenical councils, and that there were further western councils of bishops, all of which set forth doctrine and rules for the Church. Also, it cannot be denied that fixed liturgies for divine worship evolved and that a large body of ecclesiastical rules (canons) grew up within the Church.

So by the end of the Middle Ages the Church was supported by a vast system of external authority and there was an implicit claim that the whole system was directed by Christ the Lord through the hierarchy of church officers, from the Pope down to the local bishop or priest. The Protestant Reformation may be seen as a challenge to this claim.

In the last chapter we observed the different attitudes in Roman Catholicism and in Protestantism towards the scriptures and their interpretation. This background should be kept in mind as we now turn to examine the question: How does Christ the Lord exercise his authority in his Church, which possesses and venerates the sacred Scriptures of the Old and New Testament?

Pastoral oversight

Protestants readily accepted that the people of God meeting in their parish churches needed pastors and teachers. They believed that Christ the Lord still gave such gifts to his Church. The Church's duty was to look carefully for evidence of a divine call and gift in those who offered themselves for, or were available for, the pastoral ministry. According to the *Augsburg Confession* (1530), 'No man should publicly in the Church teach, or administer the sacraments, except he be rightly called' by God and the Church (Article XIV).

Further, in Part II of the *Confession*, the reform of ecclesiastical and episcopal powers is described. This should continue to be based on the distinction between that which is given by divine right (from Christ the Lord) and what is allowed or required by human right (by decision of the Church or the secular government). By divine right (or 'the power of the keys', in the language of Matthew 16:19), 'the power of the bishops, by the rule of the gospel, is a power or commandment from God, of preaching the gospel, of remitting or retaining sins, and of administering the sacraments.' Thus, bishops who possessed secular power should not claim that this was part of the authority they had received from Christ; similarly, monks should not regard their vows as something required by God but only as a requirement of human authority.

Moving from Germany and the Lutheran community to Switzerland and the Reformed community, we find the following in the 1536 *First Helvetic Confession*:

16. Concerning the Authority of the Church The authority to preach God's Word and to tend the flock of the Lord, which properly speaking is the office of the keys, prescribes one pattern of life for all men whether of high or lowly station. Since it is commanded by God, it is a high and sacred trust which should not be violated. This administrative power should not be conferred upon anyone unless he has first been found and acknowledged to be qualified and fit for the office by divine calling and election and by those who after careful deliberation have been appointed and elected as a committee of the Church for that purpose.

17. Concerning the Election of Ministers of the Church No one should be charged or entrusted with this office and ministry unless he has first been found and acknowledged by the ministers and elders of the Church, and also by those Christian rulers elected to such office on behalf of the Church, to be well instructed in the Holy Scriptures and in the knowledge of the will of God, blameless in piety and purity of life, and zealous and fervent in promoting the honour and name of Christ with diligence and earnestness. And because this is a true and proper election of God, it is reasonable and right that they should be recognised and accepted by the judgment of the Church and the laying on of hands by the elders.

18. Who the Shepherd and Head of the Church Is Christ Himself is the only true and proper Head and Shepherd of His Church. He gives to His Church shepherds and teachers who at His command administer the Word and office of the keys in an orderly and regular fashion, as reported above. Consequently we do not acknowledge or accept the head (of the Church) at Rome and those who are bishops in name only.

The Western Mediaeval Church's claim that the Pope was the head of Christendom is presented here, as in other Protestant statements, as a claim possessing only human authority, and therefore able to be rejected. However, rejection of the claims made for the bishop of Rome was rejection of one of western society's most important beliefs. The Council of Florence had, as recently as 1439, declared:

> We define that the holy apostolic See (Rome) and the Roman Pontiff have the primacy over the whole world, and that the same Roman Pontiff is the successor of St. Peter, the prince of the apostles, and the true Vicar of Christ, the head of the whole Church, the father and teacher of all Christians; and that to him, in the person of St. Peter, was given by our Lord Jesus Christ, the full power of feeding, ruling and governing the whole Church.

The pastoral rule and oversight in the mediaeval Church can be thought of in terms of a pyramid, with the Pope at the top. Under him were the senior bishops, below them the ordinary bishops, and then finally the priests and others in holy orders. This hierarchy of order possessed the 'keys of the kingdom', being able to forgive (or not to forgive) guilty sinners and include them in (or exclude them from) the Church, the Ark of salvation.

One way in which pastoral authority had been exercised by the Church through its pastoral officers was excommunication. Here is what the *Geneva Confession* (1536) said concerning the authority of Christ, exercised within the Church by duly authorised ministers:

19. Excommunication Because there are always some who hold God and his Word in contempt, who take account of neither injunction, exhortation nor remonstrance, thus requiring greater chastisement, we hold the discipline of excommunication to be a thing holy and salutary among the faithful, since truly it was instituted by our Lord with good reason. This is in order that the wicked should not by their damnable conduct corrupt the good and dishonour our Lord, and that though proud they may turn to penitence. Therefore we believe that it is expedient according to the ordinance of God that all manifest idolaters, blasphemers, murderers, thieves, lewd persons, false witnesses, seditionmongers, quarrellers, those guilty of defamation or assault, drunkards, dissolute livers, when they have been duly admonished and if they do not make amendment, be separated from the communion of the faithful until their repentance is known.

20. Ministers of the Word We recognise no other pastors in the Church than faithful pastors of the Word of God, feeding the sheep of Jesus Christ on the one hand with instruction, admonition, consolation, exhortation, deprecation; and on the other resisting all false doctrines and deceptions of the devil, without mixing with the pure doctrine of the Scriptures their dreams or their foolish imaginings. To these we accord no other power or authority but to conduct, rule, and govern the people of God committed to them by the same Word, in which they have power to command, defend, promise, and warn, and without which they neither can nor ought to attempt anything. As we receive the true ministers of the Word of God as messengers and ambassadors of God, it is necessary to listen to them as to him himself, and we hold their ministry to be a commission from God necessary in the Church. On the other hand we hold that all seductive and false prophets, who abandon the purity of the Gospel and deviate to their own inventions, ought not at all to be suffered or maintained, who are not the pastors they pretend, but rather, like ravening wolves, ought to be hunted and ejected from the people of God.

The Genevan minister had, before beginning his task, to be examined and approved for his ministry by the congregation and their pastors. By contrast, in the mediaeval Church the decision about who should be ordained rested with the hierarchy alone.

In its 1563 decree on the sacrament of order (the role of the ordained ministry), the Council of Trent merely repeated the received doctrine of the mediaeval Church. It added various condemnations of certain errors considered to exist within Protestantism. Here are some extracts from the decree, entitled 'The true and catholic doctrine concerning the sacrament of order':

The holy Synod declares that, besides the other ecclesiastical degrees, bishops, who have succeeded to the place of the Apostles, principally belong to this hierarchical order; that they are placed . . . by the Holy Ghost, to rule the Church of God; that they are superior to priests; administer the sacrament of Confirmation; ordain the ministers of the Church; and that they can perform very many other things; over which functions others of an inferior order have no power. Furthermore, the sacred and holy Synod teaches, that, in the ordination of bishops, priests, and of the other orders, neither the consent, nor vocation, nor authority, whether of the people, or of any civil power or magistrate whatsoever, is required in such wise as that, without this, the ordination is invalid: yea rather doth it decree, that all those who, being only called and instituted by the people, or by the civil power and magistrate, ascend to the exercise of these ministrations, and those who of their own rashness assume them to themselves, are not ministers of the Church, but are to be looked upon as thieves and robbers, who have not entered by the door.

So Protestant ministers, it is stated, are not true ministers or priests of the Church.

This is a strong assertion not only of the divine appointment of the basic threefold ministry of bishop, priest and deacon, but also of the claim that the Church exists because of the ordained ministry. Some Protestants were prepared to continue in their Churches the historic, threefold ordained ministry; but they made no exaggerated claims for its origins or for its logical priority over the whole people of God. Other Protestants insisted that the distinction between bishop and priest (or elder and presbyter) had no biblical foundation, and that there should be only one level of ordained pastor.

The Church of England retained the threefold ordained ministry of bishop, priest and deacon. But it rejected the minor orders (porters, lectors, exorcists and acolytes) and the order of sub-deacon. It claimed that in retaining this basic ministry it was following the primitive Church's practice. The preface of the *Ordinal* (1552) which contains the services of ordination says this: 'It is evident unto all men, diligently reading holy Scriptures and ancient authors, that from the Apostles' time there hath been these orders of ministers in Christ's Church: bishops, priests and deacons: which offices were evermore had in such reverent estimation, that no man by his own private authority might presume to execute any of them, except he be first called, tried, examined, and known to have such qualities as were requisite for the same; and also, by public prayer, with imposition of hands, approved and admitted thereunto.' The phrase 'private authority' may be contrasted with the words the bishop is to say to the deacon when ordaining him: 'Take thou authority to execute the office of a deacon in the Church of God,' and to the priest similarly, 'Take thou authority to preach the Word of God and to administer the holy Sacraments in this congregation where thou shalt be appointed.' The authority given in ordination was seen as coming from Christ the Lord.

The point needs to be made that the difference between the Roman Catholic and Protestant Church of England positions, regarding the threefold ministry, does not concern whether or not Christ gives authority to those ordained, but rather the relationship of the ministry to the whole Church. For Roman Catholics, the order of bishops is part of the essence of being of the Church (the *esse*). Therefore the Church cannot meaningfully exist without it. And consequently, ministers who have not been ordained by genuine bishops are not truly ordained, and Churches which have lost or rejected the historic order of bishops are not truly Churches. In contrast to this, the English reformers considered the order of bishops to belong to one of two categories: either to the *plene esse* or 'fullness of being', of the Church (by which was meant that only when the order of bishops is universal and acting in fellowship and harmony can the Church exist in the fullness of visible unity); or to its *bene esse*, or 'well being', by which was meant that though the Church can function with other forms of ordained ministry, the threefold ministry led by bishops is the best available. So it was possible for the Church of England to receive ordained Reformed and Lutheran ministers who had not been ordained by bishops but by presbyters, or pastors.

Some Lutheran Churches, like the Anglican, retained the order of bishops. All the Reformed Churches claimed that there should be no distinction in the ordained ministry except between pastors and deacons. They added one office to these two orders of ministery: that of lay elder, to rule the local congregation together with the ordained presbyter or pastor. The *Belgic Confession* of 1561 states:

XXXI. Of the Ministers, Elders, and Deacons We believe that the Ministers of God's Word, and the Elders and Deacons, ought to be chosen to their respective offices by a lawful election of the Church, with calling upon the name of the Lord, and in that order which the Word of God teacheth. Therefore every one must take heed not to intrude himself by indecent means, but is bound to wait till it shall please God to call him; that he may have testimony of his calling; and be certain and assured that it is of the Lord.

As for the Ministers of God's Word, they have equally the same power and authority wheresoever they are, as they are all Ministers of Christ, the only universal Bishop, and the only Head of the Church.

Moreover, that this holy ordinance of God may not be violated or slighted, we say that every one ought to esteem the Ministers of God's Word and the Elders of the Church very highly for their work's sake, and be at peace with them without murmuring, strife, or contention, as much as possible.

XXXII. Of the Order and Discipline of the Church In the mean time we believe, though it is useful and beneficial, that those who are rulers of the Church institute and establish certain ordinances among themselves for maintaining the body of the Church; yet they ought studiously to take care that they do not depart from those things which Christ, our only master, hath instituted. And, therefore, we reject all human inventions, and all laws which man would introduce into the worship of God, thereby to bind and compel the conscience in any manner whatever.

Therefore we admit only of that which tends to nourish and preserve concord and unity, and to keep all men in obedience to God. For this purpose excommunication or church discipline is requisite, with the several circumstances belonging to it, according to the Word of God.

XXX. Concerning the Government of, and Offices in, the Church We believe that this true Church must be governed by the spiritual policy which our Lord has taught us in his Word — namely, that there must be Ministers or Pastors to preach the Word of God, and to administer the Sacraments; also elders and deacons, who, together with the pastors, form the council of the Church; that by these means the true religion may be preserved, and the true doctrine every where propagated, likewise transgressors punished and restrained by spiritual means; also that the poor and distressed may be relieved and comforted, according to their necessities. By these means every thing will be carried on in the Church with good order and decency, when faithful men are chosen, according to the rule prescribed by St. Paul to Timothy (1 Tim.3).

It will be observed how the authority of Christ the Lord is seen as being expressed in the rightful actions of duly appointed ministers.

Other Presbyterian, Congregational and Baptist Confessions of Faith could be quoted to demonstrate the general acceptance that Christ appointed one basic order of ordained pastor — the minister of Word and sacrament — and the further office of deacon. Some Churches within the Reformed tradition have allowed certain men called to the ordained ministry to be primarily teachers (through the gifts of Christ), and so have called them 'doctors'. Some branches of Lutheranism have accepted an office of teacher in the Church, but have not given teachers the right of presiding at the Lord's Supper.

And so though Protestantism generally rejects the high Roman Catholic claims concerning the divine authority of bishops and the absolute necessity of distinguishing bishops from priests, there is no consensus concerning how Christ's gifts are expressed in terms of offices and officers in the local and larger units of the Church. There is however agreement that Christ's authority is expressed in the work of preaching the Word, administering the sacraments, and exercising pastoral oversight. The Anglican Communion of Churches, with certain parts of Lutheranism, appear to be nearest to the Church of Rome in terms of their understanding of how Christ's authority is exercised in the Church. But we shall see below that even they find they cannot accept the excessive claims made on behalf of one bishop — the bishop of Rome — within the Church.

The authority of synods

Every Protestant Church of the sixteenth century, and all later Protestant denominations, have used regular or occasional assemblies, synods, councils or conferences in order to set forth the doctrines they hold and the practice they follow. Where a Church has a close relationship with the State the help of the head of State, or the government, has been enlisted. The Confessions of Faith to which we are referring came out of such meetings.

A certain authority, therefore, was recognised as existing in a specific national part of the Church, to set forth authoritative teaching, to judge in controversies and to authorise certain rites and ceremonies. Article XX of the Church of England states:

> *XX. Of the Authority of the Church* The Church hath power to decree Rites or Ceremonies, and authority in Controversies of Faith: And yet it is not lawful for the Church to ordain any thing that is contrary to God's Word written, neither may it so expound one place of Scripture, that it be repugnant to another. Wherefore, although the Church be a witness and a keeper of holy Writ, yet, as it ought not to decree any thing against

the same, so besides the same ought it not to enforce any thing to be believed for necessity of Salvation.

Yet a synod or council can make mistakes, even when doing its business in sincerity and with prayer. In the words of Article XXI, both general councils and national synods 'may err and sometimes have erred'. The ancient churches of Jerusalem, Alexandria and Antioch are said to have erred: 'so also the Church of Rome hath erred, not only in their living and manner of ceremonies but also in matters of faith' (Article XIX). There is no such thing as the infallibility of the Church, of councils or synods, or of bishops of the Church. All doctrine is reformable, all practice changeable, in the light of the Word of God. This is a fundamental Protestant position, which has always been affirmed, even if it has not always been followed!

In 1647, the *Westminster Confession of Faith* gave the classic Presbyterian account of the place and authority of synods.

Of Synods and Councils

1. For the better government, and further edification of the Church, there ought to be such assemblies as are commonly called Synods or Councils.

2. As magistrates may lawfully call a synod of ministers, and other fit persons, to consult and advise with, about matters of religion; so, if magistrates be open enemies to the Church, the ministers of Christ, of themselves, by virtue of their office, or they, with other fit persons upon delegation from their Churches, may meet together in such assemblies.

3. It belongeth to synods and councils, ministerially to determine controversies of faith, and cases of conscience; to set down rules and directions for the better ordering of the public worship of God, and government of His Church; to receive complaints in cases of

maladministration, and authoritatively to determine the same: which decrees and determinations, if consonant to the Word of God, are to be received with reverence and submission; not only for their agreement with the Word, but also for the power whereby they are made, as being an ordinance of God appointed thereunto in His Word.

4. All synods or councils, since the Apostles' times, whether general or particlar, may err; and many have erred. Therefore they are not to be made the rule of faith, or practice; but to be used as a help in both.

5. Synods and councils are to handle, or conclude nothing, but that which is ecclesiastical: and are not to intermeddle with civil affairs which concern the commonwealth, unless by way of humble petition in cases extraordinary; or, by way of advice, for satisfaction of conscience, if they be thereunto required by the civil magistrate.

('Magistrates' means those who have civil authority in the State or the nation.)

Where a congregational form of church government exists and the authority of Christ the King is seen as existing directly in and through the local congregation, the need for synods is still accepted. The Congregational *Savoy Declaration of Faith and Order* (1658) (a revised form of the *Westminster Confession* for the use of congregationally-governed churches) makes the following statement on synods:

. . . It is according to the mind of Christ, that many churches holding communion together, do by their messengers meet in a synod or council, to consider and give their advice in, or about that matter in difference, to be reported to all the churches concerned; howbeit these synods so assembled are not entrusted with any churchpower, properly so-called, or with any jurisdiction over the churches themselves, to exercise any censures, either over churches or persons, or to impose their determinations on the church or officers.

This is Article XXVI; the next Article denies that any authority from Christ is vested in any synod or hierarchy of synods.

So we see that there is within Protestantism a division of opinion as to whether or not the authority of Christ is exercised outside the local Church and its appointed officers. The congregational view (represented in Independent and Baptist churches) welcomes meetings between local churches but claims that such meetings have no jurisdiction. The Presbyterian (together with the Anglican, Lutheran and Methodist) sees the need for national or regional synods to which, they believe, Christ gives a limited authority and jurisdiction. It is important to note, however, that in all forms of Protestant church government, those who are not ordained have a part to play and thus a share in the means by which the Lord Christ governs his churches.

We must now turn to examine the authority of episcopal synods within the Church of Rome. To do this, we shall also have to examine the claims made for the authority of the Pope, because the two are seen as belonging to each other. In Chapter 3 of the *Dogmatic Constitution of the Church* (November 1964) from the Second Vatican Council, the following claims are made for the authority of the bishops as they act together and under the bishop of Rome.

22. Just as, by the Lord's will, St. Peter and the other apostles constituted one apostolic college, so in a similar way the Roman Pontiff as the successor of Peter, and the bishops as the successors of the apostles are joined together. The collegial nature and meaning of the episcopal order found expression in the very ancient practice by which bishops appointed the world over were linked with one another and with the Bishop

of Rome by the bonds of unity, charity, and peace; also, in the conciliar assemblies which made common judgments about more profound matters in decisions reflecting the views of many. The ecumenical councils held through the centuries clearly attest this collegial aspect.

And it continues:

But the college or body of bishops has no authority unless it is simultaneously conceived of in terms of its head, the Roman Pontiff, Peter's successor, and without any lessening of his power of primacy over all, pastors as well as the general faithful. For in virtue of his office, that is, as Vicar of Christ and pastor of the whole Church, the Roman Pontiff has full, supreme, and universal power over the Church. And he can always exercise this power freely.

The order of bishops is the successor to the college of the apostles in teaching authority and pastoral rule; or, rather, in the episcopal order the apostolic body continues without a break. Together with its head, the Roman Pontiff, and never without the head, the episcopal order is the subject of supreme and full power over the universal Church. But this power can be exercised only with the consent of the Roman Pontiff. For our Lord made Simon Peter alone the rock and key-bearer of the Church (cf. Matt. 16:18–19), and appointed him shepherd of the whole flock (cf. John 21:15 ff.).

Later, concerning the whole number of bishops, it is claimed:

The supreme authority with which this college is empowered over the whole Church is exercised in a solemn way through an ecumenical council. A council is never ecumenical unless it is confirmed or at least accepted as such by the successor of Peter. It is the prerogative of the Roman Pontiff to convoke these councils, to preside over them, and to confirm them. The same collegiate power can be exercised in union with the Pope by the bishops living in all parts of the world, provided that the head of the college calls them to collegiate action, or at least so approves or freely accepts the united action of the dispersed bishops, that it is made a true collegiate act.

The Second Vatican Council, without altering in any way the traditional claims concerning the authority of the Pope, improved upon the First Vatican Council by emphasising the authority of all bishops acting together as a college.

In the *Dogmatic Constitution of the Church of God* (July 1870) the First Vatican Council explained in detail the primacy of the Bishop of Rome as the successor of Peter, who was the first among the apostles. Then it set forth the doctrine of papal infallibility:

And so, faithfully keeping to the tradition received from the beginning of the Christian faith, for the glory of God our Saviour, for the exaltation of the Catholic religion, and for the salvation of Christian peoples, We, with the approval of the sacred Council, teach and define: It is a divinely revealed dogma that the Roman Pontiff, when he speaks *ex cathedra*, that is, when, acting in the office of shepherd and teacher of all Christians, he defines, by virtue of his supreme apostolic authority, a doctrine concerning faith or morals to be held by the universal Church, possesses through the divine assistance promised to him in the person of Blessed Peter, the infallibility with which the divine Redeemer willed His Church to be endowed in defining the doctrine concerning faith or morals; and that such definitions of the Roman Pontiff are there- fore irreformable of themselves, not because of the consent of the Church (*ex sese, non autem ex consensu ecclesiae*).

What precisely this doctrine of papal infallibility means has been, and is, much discussed among Roman Catholic scholars. It has only been exercised on rare occasions, the most recent being the dogma of the Assumption of the Blessed Virgin Mary (1950).

Clearly there is a wide gulf here between Protestants and Roman Catholics. To accept that the Pope in Rome is the bishop of Rome, having only the pastoral oversight of his diocese, is one thing, and could possibly be accepted by many Protestants. What is claimed over and above this is quite another thing, and it is this that constitutes the problem. The papers of the North American Roman Catholic-Lutheran commission reveal that this gulf exists, even when ecumenically-minded theologians are the participants.[1] Further, the final report of the international Roman Catholic/Anglican Commission entitled *Authority in the Church II* (1981) clearly reveals that even if a way can be found of regarding the bishop of Rome as primate (the senior presiding bishop in western Christendom), the doctrine of papal infallibility is a problem yet to be resolved.

The Magisterium and personal morality

Before leaving the subject of the authority of the Pope and the college of bishops we must look briefly at the question of their authority over the faithful in issues of personal morality. This has been the subject of recent public discussion because of papal pronouncements, in documents and in public speeches, on birth control and contraception.

The Church as teacher is given the title of the *Magisterium*. It is held that the authority of the Magisterium by which it teaches what is necessary to be believed for the purpose of salvation rests in the Pope, either acting with the college of bishops or speaking infallibly as Pope. The beliefs in question concern teaching, about the character of God, the identity and work of Jesus, the Holy Spirit, the Church and the Sacraments. The commandment to love God, one's neighbour and one's enemy, according to Jesus' example, is included in such doctrine.

But what is the status of pronouncement by the Pope, which takes the general principle of love and applies it to very particular and personal matters? Is it to be seen as the only valid way of understanding the will of God in the specific situation?

Consider the topic of Christian marriage and the purpose of sexual intercourse. In 1968, Pope Paul VI issued his encyclical *Humanae Vitae*, which said many splendid things about marriage. But in this document he also expressed his judgement regarding contraception. Section 14:

14. Therefore we base our words on the first principle of a human and Christian doctrine of marriage when we are obliged once more to declare that the direct interruption of the generative process already begun and, above all, direct abortion, even for therapeutic reasons, are to be absolutely excluded as lawful means of controlling the birth of children.

Equally to be condemned, as the Magisterium of the Church has affirmed on various occasions, is direct sterilization, whether of the man or of the woman, whether permanent or temporary.

Similarly excluded is any action, which either before, at the moment of, or after sexual intercourse, is specifically intended to prevent procreation — whether as an end or as a means.

Neither is it valid to argue, as a justification for sexual intercourse which is deliberately contraceptive, that a lesser evil is to be preferred to a greater one, or that such intercourse would merge with the normal relations of past and future to form a single entity, and so be qualified by exactly the same moral goodness as these. Though it is true that sometimes it is lawful to tolerate a lesser moral evil in order to avoid a greater or in order to promote a greater good, it is never lawful, even for the gravest reasons, to do evil that good may come of it — in other words, to intend positively something which intrinsically contradicts the moral order, and which must therefore be judged unworthy of man, even though the intention is to protect or promote the welfare of an individual, of a family or of society in general. Consequently it is a serious error to think that a whole married life of otherwise normal relations can justify sexual intercourse which is deliberately contraceptive and so intrinsically wrong.

Here contraception is placed on the same level as abortion and sterilization.

The statements regarding contraception caused a great crisis for authority within the Church. The Pope was requiring the faithful to adopt an attitude and a pattern of behaviour which many believed in their conscience to be wrong. The Vicar of Christ was directing them to do what, instinctively, they believed not to be God's will. Further, they discovered that many theologians and priests shared their viewpoint. The situation now is that the majority of married couples within the Roman Catholic Church in western society use some form of contraception.

Theologically, this crisis of authority helped many Roman Catholics to sort out the difference between the Magisterium teaching (infallibly) what is to be believed for salvation, and teaching what it believes to be the right, practical application of the divine law of love in specific situations. Roman Catholics must believe what the Church teaches in the doctrine of salvation; over this, there can be no question. However, they are to follow their consciences in matters of personal or even social morality. Of course their consciences must be informed by the Holy Scriptures, by Church tradition, by the pronouncements of the Pope and bishops, by scientific information and other forms of knowledge. But in the final analysis the priority of conscience has to be followed.

It is true that many conservative priests and laity tend to look upon the official pronouncements of the Papacy as being only on one level, all possessing equal authority. However, most priests and laity now tend to distinguish carefully, between the Magisterium pronouncing infallibly concerning the content of the Faith, and giving advice (in a rather authoritative style!) concerning morality. In fact, in matters of personal and social morality there is no basic difference between the view of the enlightened Roman Catholic and the Protestant. Both agree that conscience is primary, and that it has to be informed by the best available knowledge.

It would be wrong to leave the impression that all Papal Encyclicals on social and personal morality are out of touch with real situations and people. For example, not a few Protestants, along with most Roman Catholics, think that *Familiaris Consortio* (1981) is a superb statement on family life. Protestants have often lacked clear leadership in social ethics, but in contrast Roman Catholics have had much excellent teaching in recent decades.

1. *Papal primacy and the universal Church: Lutherans and Catholics in dialogue* (Minneapolis, 1974).

6: How are you justified?

The doctrine of 'justification by faith alone' is particularly associated with the German reformer Martin Luther. It is present in virtually everything he wrote, but especially in his *Preface to the Epistle to the Romans*, *The Freedom of a Christian man*, and *Commentary on Galatians*. The best way of describing the doctrine is to say that it restates the teaching of St. Augustine of Hippo (354–430), in the light of Luther's own careful study of the writings of St. Paul. The doctrine became for Luther the article of faith by which the Church stands or falls. With this doctrine he challenged the Pope and the whole Church, and in the light of it he called for reformation.

For Luther, the doctrine expressed the gospel. It brought together the God of grace and sinful, condemned man. It asserted that salvation is entirely by divine mercy and divine initiative. God in Christ has made salvation possible. Justification rests wholly on the grace of God revealed and given to sinful man in Jesus Christ, Saviour and Mediator. The situation of humanity shows that grace is desperately needed. Not only is mankind guilty before God — the just judge — in that mankind has broken God's moral law; but also we are incapable of helping ourselves because our will is enslaved. We can do nothing whatsoever to deserve salvation, far less obtain it, because we are in bondage to sin. This is the theme of Luther's *The bondage of the will* (1525).

For Luther, doctrine cannot be separated from personal experience. The doctrine of justification became clear to him after he had searched long and painfully for a gracious God who would accept him as he was rather than condemn him for his sins. This search involved his whole being, and included meticulous study of the Bible and the works of the Fathers. In particular it involved a study of the meaning of the righteousness and justice of God, as Paul uses the concept in his Letter to the Romans, notably at 1:16-17:

> For I am not ashamed of the gospel: for it is the power of God unto salvation to every one that believeth; to the Jew first and also to the Greek. For therein is revealed a righteousness of God by faith: as it is written, But the righteous shall live by faith.

Luther explained:

> I greatly longed to understand Paul's Epistle to the Romans and nothing stood in the way but that one expression, 'the justice of God', because I took it to mean that justice whereby God is just and deals justly in punishing the unjust. My situation was that, although an impeccable monk, I stood before God as a sinner troubled in conscience, and I had no confidence that my merit would assuage him. Therefore I did not love a just and angry God, but rather hated and murmured against him. Yet I clung to the dear Paul and had a great yearning to know what he meant.
>
> Night and day I pondered until I saw the connection between the justice of God and the statement that 'the just shall live by faith.' Then I grasped that the justice of God is that righteousness by which through grace and sheer mercy God justifies us through faith. Thereupon I felt myself to be reborn and to have gone through open doors into paradise. The whole of Scripture took on a new meaning, and whereas before the 'justice of God' had filled me with hate, now it became to me inexpressibly sweet in greater love. This passage of Paul became to me a gate to heaven . . .

It need hardly be added that this 'discovery' changed the direction of his life, and led to him becoming an outstanding reformer of the Church.

Early Protestant statements

Following the lead of Luther the *Augsburg Confession* (1530) claimed that within the evangelical Church in Germany, 'they teach that men cannot be justified in the sight of God by their own strength, merits or works, but that they are justified freely on account of Christ through faith, when they believe that they are received into grace and that their sins are remitted on account of Christ who made satisfaction for sins on our behalf by his death' (Article IV).

Here we find the fundamentals of the Protestant doctrine. The righteousness by which Christians are justified and made members of the family of God is that of Christ — the same Christ who died for our sins and is now exalted to the Father's right hand. This righteousness of our Saviour is reckoned to us, when we truly believe and trust God as the God of mercy and grace. Justification is totally by grace. It cannot be gained by human effort. Even faith is a gift of God.

Within the Reformed Churches, which also learned from Luther how to understand Paul's teaching on righteousness and faith, the same doctrine was set forth. The *First Confession of Basel* (1534) reads:

> *IX. Concerning Faith and Works* We confess that there
> is forgiveness of sins through faith in Jesus Christ the
> crucified. Although this faith is continually exercised,
> signalised, and thus confirmed by works of love yet do
> we not ascribe to works, which are the fruit of faith,
> the righteousness and satisfaction for our sins. On the
> contrary we ascribe it solely to a genuine trust and faith
> in the shed blood of the Lamb of God. For we freely
> confess that all things are granted to us in Christ, Who
> is our righteousness, holiness, redemption, the way,
> the truth, the wisdom and the life. Therefore the
> works of believers are not for the satisfaction of their
> sins, but solely for the purpose of showing in some
> degree our gratitude to the Lord God for the great

kindness He has shown us in Christ.

True faith in Christ, the reformers constantly emphasised, expresses itself in faithfulness to Christ and
thankfulness to God in everyday life. This emphasis was
necessary not only for the pastoral care of their flocks but
also because Roman Catholic criticism was often intended to show that Protestants believed in faith but not
in living the holy and righteous life.

There was full recognition of the need for a salvation
which brought a right relationship with God and a
genuine love for one's neighbour through inner renewal.
The *Geneva Confession* (1536) states:

6. *Salvation in Jesus* We confess then that it is Jesus
Christ who is given to us by the Father, in order that in
him we should recover all of which in ourselves we are
deficient. Now all that Jesus Christ has done and
suffered for our redemption, we veritably hold without
any doubt, as it is contained in the Creed, which is
recited in the Church, that is to say: I believe in God
the Father Almighty, and so on.

7. *Righteousness in Jesus* Therefore we acknowledge the
things which are consequently given to us by God in
Jesus Christ: first, that being in our own natures
enemies of God and subjects of his wrath and
judgment, we are reconciled with him and received
again in grace through the intercession of Jesus Christ,
so that by his righteousness and guiltlessness we have
remission of our sins, and by the shedding of his blood
we are cleansed and purified from all our stains.

8. *Regeneration in Jesus* Second, we acknowledge that
by his Spirit we are regenerated into a new spiritual
nature. That is to say that the evil desires of our flesh
are mortified by grace, so that they rule us no longer.
On the contrary, our will is rendered conformable to
God's will, to follow in his way and to seek that is

pleasing to him. Therefore we are by him delivered from the servitude of sin, under whose power we were of ourselves held captive, and by this deliverance we are made capable and able to do good works and not otherwise.

9. Remission of sins always necessary for the faithful
Finally, we acknowledge that this regeneration is so affected in us that, until we slough off this mortal body, there remains always in us much imperfection and infirmity, so that we always remain poor and wretched sinners in the presence of God. And, however much we ought day by day to increase and grow in God's righteousness, there will never be plenitude or perfection while we live here. Thus we always have need of the mercy of God to obtain the remission of our faults and offences. And so we ought always to look for our righteousness in Jesus Christ and not at all in ourselves, and in him be confident and assured, putting no faith in our works.

Here we encounter the distinction between what came to be called *justification* (God's declaration in heaven) and *sanctification* (God's work within those who truly believe). They were seen in all the Churches of the Reformation as two inseparable aspects of the one grace of God, who saves those who are united to his Incarnate Son.

The Council of Trent

The *Decree on Justification (1547)* was one of the earliest authoritative declarations of the Council, and it is much more than a mere condemnation of Protestant teaching. It is a sophisticated theological document.

Chapter 1, in recalling the earlier decree on original sin, declares that neither by man's natural powers nor by the moral law is he to be justified before God. In contrast, chapter 2 points to the Incarnate Son, Jesus

Christ, as the Saviour of both Jew and Gentile.

Chapter 3 affirms that those to whom the merit of the passion of Christ is communicated are justified: 'seeing that, in that new birth (John 3:3–6), there is bestowed upon them, through the merit of his passion, the grace whereby they are made just'. Justification means to be *made*, not *declared*, just (righteous).

In chapter 4, justification is defined as being 'a translation, from that state wherein man is born a child of Adam, to the state of grace, and of the adoption of the sons of God, through the second Adam, Jesus Christ, our Saviour. And this translation, since the promulgation of the Gospel, cannot be effected, without the laver of regeneration. . . . .' Justification is a process which begins with the event of baptism, the 'laver of regeneration'.

Chapter 5 explains the necessity of preparation for justification in adults. By the illumination of the Spirit the heart of man is turned towards God but man must respond positively and cooperate with the leading of the Spirit. 'He is not able by his own free will, without the grace of God, to move himself unto justice in his sight.'

More information on preparation for justification (which includes regeneration) is provided in Chapter six. Prompted and assisted by the Holy Spirit sinners believe God's revealed promises of salvation and they turn towards the Lord, knowing that he is the God of mercy; 'and they begin to love him as the fountain of all justice; and are therefore moved against sins by a certain hatred and detestation, to wit, by that penitence which must be performed before baptism, to begin a new life and to keep the commandments of God'.

Chapter seven is one of the more important chapters and begins by defining justification as 'not remission of sins merely, but also the sanctification and renewal of the inward man, through the voluntary reception of the grace, and the gifts, whereby man of unjust becomes just, and of an enemy a friend, so that he may be an heir according to hope of life everlasting.'

Then in mediaeval style the causes of justification — 'final, efficient, meritorious, instrumental and formal' — are explained.

Of this Justification the causes are these: the final cause indeed is the glory of God and of Jesus Christ, and life everlasting; while the efficient cause is a merciful God who washes and sanctifies gratuitously, signing, and anointing with the holy Spirit of promise, who is the pledge of our inheritance; but the meritorious cause is his most beloved only-begotten, our Lord Jesus Christ, who, when we were enemies, for the exceeding charity wherewith he loved us, merited Justification for us by his most holy Passion on the wood of the cross, and made satisfaction for us unto God the Father; the instrumental cause is the sacrament of baptism, which is the sacrament of faith, without which (faith) no man was ever justified; lastly, the alone formal cause is the justice of God, not that whereby he himself is just, but that whereby he maketh us just, that, to wit, with which we, being endowed by him, are renewed in the spirit of our mind, and we are not only reputed, but are truly called, and are just, receiving justice within us, each one according to his own measure, which the Holy Ghost distributes to every one as he wills, and according to each one's proper disposition and co-operation. For, although no one can be just, but he to whom the merits of the Passion of our Lord Jesus Christ are communicated, yet is this done in the said justification of the impious, when by the merit of that same most holy Passion, the charity of God is poured forth, by the Holy Spirit, in the hearts of those that are justified, and is inherent therein: whence, man, through Jesus Christ, in whom he is ingrafted, receives, in the said justification, together with the remission of sins, all these (gifts) infused at once, faith, hope and charity. For faith, unless hope and charity be added thereto, neither unites man perfectly with

Christ, nor makes him a living member of his body.

Here is the heart of the Tridentine doctrine. The 'formal cause' is inherent righteousness, imparted to sinners; while true faith is always accompanied by hope and charity.

Chapter eight acknowledges the primacy of faith. 'Faith is the beginning of human salvation, the foundation, and the root of all justification.' Yet faith does not merit salvation. It merely goes before justification.

A polemical note enters in Chapter nine, which is 'Against the vain confidence of heretics'. This confidence (of Protestants) is the assurance of justification which they claim to enjoy within their souls. In contrast, the received Catholic theology teaches that, 'for even as no pious person ought to doubt of the mercy of God, of the merit of Christ, and of the virtue and efficacy of the sacraments, even so each one, when he regards himself and his own weakness and indisposition, may have fear and apprehension touching his own grace; seeing that no one can know with a certainty of faith, which cannot be subject to error, that he has obtained the grace of God'.

Justification, states chapter ten, is the process of becoming just and is thus to be increased within the faithful. 'They, through the observance of the commandments of God and of the Church, faith co-operating with good works, increase in that justice which they have received through the grace of Christ, and are still further justified.' The need to keep God's commandments continually is emphasised in chapter eleven. 'Whoso are the sons of God love Christ; but they who love him keep his commandments . . . . which assuredly with the divine help they can do.' Those who persist will never be forsaken by God: 'for God forsakes not those who have been once justified by his grace, unless he be first forsaken by them.' It is a rash presumption, however, as chapter twelve declares, for a Christian to presume that he is surely one of the elect. In fact, as chapter thirteen makes clear, perseverance is a gift of God and so 'let those who think themselves to stand, take heed lest they fall, and, with fear and trembling work out their salvation in labours, in watchings, in almsdeeds, in prayers and oblations, in fastings and chastity. . . .'

Chapter fourteen is concerned with the recovery of the state of justification through the sacrament of penance by those who have fallen from grace. In the following chapter it is claimed that 'the received grace of justification is lost, not only by infidelity whereby even faith itself is lost, but also by any other mortal sin whatever, though faith be not lost.' The distinction between mortal (or deadly or grave) and venial sin is common in Roman Catholic theology. While the former deprives the Christian of sanctifying grace the latter does not. Venial sins have been called 'daily sins' or 'light sins'. The purpose of the sacrament of penance is to forgive sins committed after baptism, and to restore the penitent to the position that obtained after baptism.

The final chapter (xvi) describes the merit of good works. 'Life eternal is to be proposed to those working well unto the end and hoping in God, both as a grace mercifully promised to the sons of God through Jesus Christ, and as a reward which is according to the promise of God himself to be faithfully rendered to their good works and merits.' And it continues:

For, whereas Jesus Christ himself continually infuses his virtue into the said justified, — as the head into the members, and the vine into the branches, — and this virtue always precedes and accompanies and follows their good works, which without it could not in any wise be pleasing and meritorious before God, — we must believe that nothing further is wanting to the justified, to prevent their being accounted to have, by those very works which have been done in God, fully satisfied the divine law according to the state of this life, and to have truly merited eternal life, to be obtained also in its (due) time, if so be, however, that they depart in grace.

The chapter gives explanations of 'infused' and 'inherent' righteousness (justice): 'Neither is our own justice established as our own from ourselves; nor is the justice of God ignored or repudiated: for that justice which is called ours, because that we are justified from its being inherent in us, that same is [the justice] of God, because that it is infused into us of God, through the merit of Christ.'

Thirty-three canons end the decree, each beginning 'If any one saith . . .' and concluding 'Let him be anathema.' These serve to reinforce what has already been taught.

The *Decree*'s teaching represents, not merely a rejection of Lutheran theology, but a restatement of the old Western Catholic doctrine of justification as expounded by Augustine and confirmed by Aquinas. Naturally the existence of Protestantism affects the way the subject is approached, but the chapters, more than being simply a rebuttal of Protestant teaching, represents a return to Augustine's teaching, by setting aside later mediaeval accretions and errors. The sixteen chapters can be said to comprise a positive exposition of the doctrine, and the thirty-three canons an exposure of 'errors' concerning justification detected by the Roman theologians in the mid-sixteenth century European Churches.

Let us now summarise the main features of the Roman doctrine of justification.

1. Justification is both an event and a process. An unrighteous man becomes a righteous man. Becoming a child of God in baptism and having the remission of sins, the Christian is made righteous. (If during this process he should lose faith or fall away, he may be restored through the sacrament of penance.)

2. Justification occurs because of the 'infusion' of the grace of God into the soul, whereby inherent righteousness becomes one of the soul's characteristics.

3. This imparted, 'infused' righteousness is described as the 'formal cause' of justification. The 'meritorous cause' is Christ's passion and death.

4. The believer will only know for certain that he is justified at the end of the process. In the meantime, his constant duty is to co-operate with the grace of God given to him.

It is true that the *Decree* of the Council of Trent established Roman Catholic doctrine and excluded certain debates. It is not true that it prohibited all further exploration of the theme. Subsequent explorations, however, have concerned secondary aspects of the doctrine, not its central tenets — for example, over what it means precisely to co-operate with divine grace; not over what the 'formal Cause' is. So though discussion continues to this present time, there has been no further official statement of the doctrine, and no document on the subject was issued by Vatican II.

Later Protestant statements

After the *Decree* was published in 1547, Protestant writers engaged in controversy with Roman theologians had to face the challenge which this document presented. This meant in practice that Protestant books and statements emphasised two primary points of difference and several secondary ones.

They held that the formal cause (the reason a thing is what it is) of justification is the (external) righteousness of Christ, who is in heaven. This righteousness is 'outside', or separate from, the believer; for it is where Christ is, seated at the Father's right hand. They denied that the gracious internal work of the Spirit, creating a new heart in the believer, could be regarded as the formal cause.

Furthermore they distinguished very clearly between 'justification', meaning what God the Father declares to be true in his heavenly court, and 'sanctification', meaning what God the Spirit achieves in the life of a believer over that lifetime. But they insisted that the two always went together; somebody who is truly justified is actually being sanctified. They denied that justification means 'to be made righteous' and that sanctification is part of justification. Rather, they claimed that justification means 'to be declared righteous'; and thus, the related and accompanying work of God is sanctification, the actual process of becoming righteous.

There were other points of difference, including the following. There was the question of what the 'instrumental cause' — the means — of salvation was. Roman Catholics claimed that it was the sacrament of holy Baptism, while Protestants claimed that it was saving faith — itself a gift of God. There was also the question, raised at the Council of Trent, of whether a sinner who believes and is baptised can ever really be sure that he will go to heaven. Roman Catholics said that it was not possible; Protestants claimed that it was possibly to be sure of one's justification and so to be sure one was going to heaven.

Most of the major Protestant doctrinal confessions of faith in the century following contained statements on justification. The Lutherans addressed themselves to the question not only in the light of the teaching of Trent but that of their own internal debates as well, in Article 3 of the *Formula of Concord* (1577). The *Thirty-Nine Articles* briefly explains justification: 'We are accounted righteous before God only for the merit of our Lord and Saviour Jesus Christ by faith, and not for our own works or deservings.' Then Articles XII, XIII and XIV address the question of good works, and deny Roman Catholic claims concerning merit.

The developed Reformed teaching is found in the *Westminster Confession of Faith* and in the *Larger Catechism*, produced by the same divines in London in 1647. Several answers from the *Larger Catechism* express the matter as clearly, perhaps, as it can be expressed.

Q. 70 What is justification?

Justification is an act of God's free grace unto sinners, in which he pardoneth all their sins, accepteth and accounteth their persons righteous in his sight; not for any thing wrought in them, or done by them, but only for the perfect obedience and full satisfaction of Christ, by God imputed to them, and received by faith alone.

Q. 73. How doth faith justify a sinner in the sight of God?

Faith justifies a sinner in the sight of God, not because of those other graces which do always accompany it, or of good works that are the fruits of it, nor as if the grace of faith, or any act thereof, were imputed to him for justification; but only as it is an instrument by which he receiveth and applieth Christ and his righteousness.

Q. 75. What is sanctification?

Sanctification is a work of God's grace, whereby they whom God hath, before the foundation of the world, chosen to be holy, are in time, through the powerful operation of his Spirit applying the death and resurrection of Christ unto them, renewed in their whole man after the image of God; having the seeds of repentance unto life, and all other saving graces, put into their hearts, and those graces so stirred up, increased, and strengthened, as that they more and more die unto sin, and rise unto newness of life.

Q. 77. Wherein do justification and sanctification differ?

Although sanctification be inseparably joined with justification, yet they differ, in that God in justification imputeth the righteousness of Christ; in sanctification his Spirit infuseth grace, and enableth to the exercise thereof; in the former, sin is pardoned; in the other, it is subdued: the one doth equally free all believers from the revenging wrath of God, and that perfectly in this life, that they never fall into condemnation; the other is neither equal in all, nor in this life perfect in any, but growing up to perfection.

Perhaps it would be right to observe here that Roman Catholic and Protestant biblical scholars are able to come to similar conclusions concerning the meaning of such New Testament words as 'righteousness' and 'faith'. This fact appears to bring the possibility of a common approach to justification some degree nearer. The forthcoming Roman Catholic-Lutheran report from America (*Lutherans and Catholics in dialogue: Justification* [1984]) would suggest this. However, the doctrine of justification cannot be isolated from other doctrines and it will not be possible to agree on a modern statement of the meaning of justification until other, related areas are also agreed.

Finally, it may be observed that there is general agreement that Protestant reformers were correct when they argued that the Greek verb 'to justify' means 'to account or reckon as righteous' rather than 'to make righteous'. The Latin verb *justificare* had been understood ever since the fifth century to mean 'to make righteous', and this explains the commitment of the mediaeval Church and then of Roman Catholicism to the idea of 'justification' as the process of 'making just', or making righteous. However, to state this does not mean that the best way to understand 'to reckon as righteous' is by using forensic, or legal, images drawn from Roman law, as the traditional expositors have done. The Protestant tradition of teaching on justification might perhaps have been healthier, if it had made use of the legal ideas in Hebrew law rather than those of Roman law.

7: What is a sacrament?

The word 'sacrament' comes from the Latin word *sacramentum*, meaning an oath, especially the oath of a soldier declaring his allegiance. However, its meaning in the Church is much richer than that of its Latin root, since in the Latin New Testament sacramentum was used to translate the Greek word *mysterion* (which means, 'mystery'). Thus a sacrament was more than it seemed to be, and came to refer to an external, visible sign to which God joined an internal and invisible act of his grace.

From the beginning, the Church was quite sure that baptism and the Lord's supper (or Eucharist, or Mass) were commanded by Christ and could be called sacraments. However, over the centuries, there was much discussion as to which other signs could be regarded as being instituted by Christ and conveying internal and invisible grace. Towards the end of the Middle Ages, it appears that the Church in the West considered that there were seven sacraments.

The Council of Florence (1439) made the following declaration:

> There are seven sacraments of the New Law, namely, baptism, confirmation, the Eucharist, penance, extreme unction, Order and matrimony; and they differ greatly from the sacraments of the Old Law. For these did not cause grace but were only a figure of the grace that was to be given through the passion of Christ; but our sacraments both contain grace and confer it on those who receive them worthily.
>
> The first five of these are ordained to the interior spiritual perfection of the person himself; the last two are ordained to the government and the increase of the

whole Church. For by baptism we are spiritually reborn and by confirmation we grow in grace and are strengthened in the faith; being reborn and strengthened, we are nourished with the divine food of the Eucharist. If by sin we become sick in soul, we are healed spiritually by penance; we are also healed in spirit, and in body in so far as it is good for the soul, by extreme unction. Through Order the Church is governed and receives spiritual growth; through matrimony she receives bodily growth.

All these sacraments are constituted by the three elements: by things as the matter, by words as the form, and by the person of the minister conferring the sacrament with the intention of doing what the Church does. And if any one of these three is lacking, the sacrament is not effected.

Among these sacraments there are three, baptism, confirmation and Order, which imprint on the soul an indelible character, that is a certain spiritual sign distinguishing (the recipient) from others. Hence, these are not repeated for the same person. The other four, however do not imprint a character and may be repeated.

A century later the Council of Trent (1545–1563) confirmed for the Roman Catholic Church that there were seven sacraments: baptism, confirmation, the Eucharist, penance, extreme unction, Order(s), and matrimony.

Protestant teaching

Because they were committed to the principle of only requiring what Christ or the apostles had specifically commanded, the Protestant reformers rejected the teaching that there were seven sacraments. They claimed that there were certainly two, perhaps three, but certainly not seven. The rest, though important, could not be called sacraments, because they were not instituted directly by Christ with a promise of grace.

The *Augsburg Confession* (1530) describes baptism, the Lord's Supper (Mass), and confession. Of the latter the Lutherans asserted: 'It is taught among us that private absolution should be retained and not allowed to fall into disuse. However, in confession it is not necessary to enumerate all trespasses and sins, for this is impossible. Psalm 19:12, "Who can discern his errors?"' (Article XI). The same position is explained in the later *Formula of Concord* (1577). But is is debatable whether Lutherans actually regard confession as a sacrament at the same level as baptism and the Lord's Supper.

The exercise of faith was a very important part of the Lutheran concept of the work of God in sacraments. Article XIII of the *Augsberg Confession* states: 'It is taught among us that the sacraments were instituted not only to be signs by which people might be identified outwardly as Christians, but that they are signs and testimonies of God's will toward us for the purpose of awakening and strengthening our faith. For this reason they require faith, and they are rightly used when they are received in faith and for the purpose of strengthening faith.'

Six years later, this statement came from the Swiss Reformed Church in the *First Helvetic Confession* (1536):

> 20. *Concerning the Power and Efficacy of the Sacraments*
> The signs, which are called sacraments, are two:
> Baptism and the Lord's Supper. These sacraments are
> significant, holy signs of sublime, secret things.
> However, they are not mere, empty signs, but consist
> of the sign and substance. For in baptism the water is
> the sign, but the substance and spiritual thing is
> rebirth and admission into the people of God. In the
> Lord's Supper the bread and wine are the signs, but
> the spiritual substance is the communion of the body
> and blood of Christ, the salvation acquired on the
> Cross, and forgiveness of sins. As the signs are bodily
> received, so these substantial, invisible and spiritual
> things are received in faith. Moreover, the entire

power, efficacy and fruit of the sacraments lies in these spiritual and substantial things.

Consequently we confess that the sacraments are not simply outward signs of Christian fellowship. On the contrary, we confess them to be signs of divine grace by which the ministers of the Church work with the Lord for the purpose and to the end which He Himself promises, offers and efficaciously provides. We confess, however, that all sanctifying and saving power is to be ascribed to God, the Lord, alone, as we said above concerning the servants of the Word.

In the same year the *Geneva Confession* taught similarly, but ended by stating that 'what is held within the realm of the Pope concerning seven sacraments, we condemn as fable and lie' (Article XIV). Three decades later, the Church of England declared that 'those five commonly-called sacraments . . . are not to be counted for sacraments of the gospel, being such as have grown partly of the corrupt following of the apostles, partly are states of life allowed in the Scriptures; but yet have not like nature of sacraments with baptism, and the Lord's Supper, for that they have not any visible sign or ceremony ordained of God' (Article XXV).

One thing is clear. Both Roman Catholics and Protestants agreed that baptism and the Lord's Supper were 'dominical' sacraments (given by the Lord). Further, their actual differences over the practice and meaning of baptism were (in comparison with other differences) minimal. Yet concerning the Lord's Supper there were some profound differences, and these have continued to be problems. Therefore, instead of looking at many different areas of difference with regard to the sacraments, we shall devote what space we have to the Eucharist.

The Eucharist

In the Mediaeval Church the Mass or Eucharist was seen

as both a sacrifice and a meal. Within the Church on earth, it perpetuated the sacrifice offered by Christ and Calvary for the sins of the world. It was also a banquet for the priests and faithful of the body and blood of Christ. In this sacrament of the altar, Christ was present through the Holy Spirit in the reality of his glorified humanity under the form of bread and wine.

At the Fourth Lateran Council (1215) the famous doctrine of transubstantiation was officially accepted and set forth in this manner:

> There is indeed one universal Church of the faithful outside which no one at all is saved, and in which the priest himself, Jesus Christ, is also the sacrifice. His body and blood are truly contained in the sacrament of the altar under the appearance of bread and wine, the bread being transubstantiated into the body by the divine power and the wine into the blood, to the effect that we receive from what is His in what He has received from what is ours [i.e. our humanity] in order that the mystery of unity may be accomplished.

Transubstantiation means that the whole bread becomes the whole body of Christ and that the whole wine becomes the whole blood of Christ. Then this is offered as a sacrifice to the Father (the sacrifice of the Mass) and to the faithful as food for their souls (the banquet of the Mass). Ordination (the sacrament of Order) gives to the priest the power to preside at Mass and be the means through which transubstantiation occurs.

The custom that the priest received both bread and wine, and the laity only bread, was confirmed by the Council of Constance (1415) when it rejected the teaching of the disciples of John Hus of Bohemia that the laity should receive the chalice. It declared that this custom of communicating only 'in one kind' was legitimate, 'for it must be firmly believed and can in no way be doubted that the body and blood of Christ are truly and integrally contained under the species of bread as well as under that of wine.' So to receive either the bread or the wine is to receive the whole Christ.

The Protestant response to the medieval doctrine of the Mass was to subject it to scriptural investigation. This led to a positive affirmation of the sacrament as a way of personal communion with Christ and to severe criticism of certain aspects of the medieval practice and doctrine.

Let us begin with the Lutheran response. Article X of the *Augsburg Confession* briefly states that 'it is taught among us that the true body and blood of Christ are really present in the Supper of our Lord under the form of bread and wine and are therefore distributed and received.' In the second half of the *Confession* the custom of giving both kinds to the laity is commended. Then there is a long section insisting that 'the Mass is observed among us with greater devotion and the more earnestness than among our opponents' and the practice of mercenary and private Masses had been stopped. At the same time 'the abominable error was condemned according to which it was taught that our Lord Christ had by his death made satisfaction only for original sin, and had instituted the Mass as a sacrifice for other sins. This transformed the Mass into a sacrifice for the living and the dead, a sacrifice by means of which sin was taken away and God was reconciled.'

Later in the century the *Formula of Concord* rejected the 'papistical transubstantiation', 'the sacrifiice of the Mass which is offered for the sins of the living and the dead', 'the sacrilege whereby one part of the sacrament only is given to the laity', and several other Roman Catholic doctrines. But it also confirmed that Lutherans 'believe, teach and confess that the body and blood of Christ are taken with the bread and wine, not only spiritually through faith, but also by the mouth . . . but after a spiritual and heavenly manner, by reason of the sacramental union.'

For the Reformed Churches the *Geneva Confession* (1536) declared both a positive faith and a critical evaluation of the medieval tradition:

16. *The Holy Supper* The Supper of our Lord is a sign
by which under bread and wine he represents the true
spiritual communion which we have in his body and
blood. And we acknowledge that according to his
ordinance it ought to be distributed in the company of
the faithful, in order that all who wish to have Jesus for
their life be partakers of it. In as much as the Mass of
the Pope was a reprobate and diabolical ordinance
subverting the mystery of the Lord's Supper, we
declare that it is execrable to us, an idolatry condemned by God; for so much is it itself regarded as a
sacrifice for the redemption of souls that the bread is in
it taken and adored as God. Besides there are other
execrable blasphemies and superstitions implied here,
and the abuse of the Word of God which is taken in
vain without profit or edification.

Here the same Protestant themes emerge. The mystery of
Holy Communion is that there is a true fellowship with
the Lord Jesus Christ and a true participation in him.
The medieval doctrine of the sacrifice of the Mass, the
concept of transubstantiation and the cultus that went
with them are condemned.

In the *Belgic Confession* (1561) There is a full statement
of the mature Reformed teaching of the meaning of the
Lord's Supper:

XXXV Of the Holy Supper of Our Lord Jesus Christ We
believe and confess that our Saviour Jesus Christ did
ordain and institute the Sacrament of the Holy Supper,
to nourish and support those whom he hath already
regenerated and incorporated into his family, which is
his Church. Now those who are regenerated have in
them a twofold life, the one bodily and temporal,
which they have from the first birth, and is common to
all men; the other spiritual and heavenly, which is
given them in their second birth, which is effected by

the word of the gospel, in the communion of the body of Christ; and this life is not common, but is peculiar to God's elect. In like manner God hath given us, for the support of the bodily and earthly life, earthly and common bread, which is subservient thereto, and is common to all men, even as life itself. But for the support of the spiritual and heavenly life which believers have, he hath sent a living bread, which descended from heaven, namely Jesus Christ, who nourishes and strengthens the spiritual life of believers, when they eat him, that is to say, when they apply and receive him by faith, in the Spirit. Christ, that he might represent unto us this spiritual and heavenly bread, hath instituted an earthly and visible bread as a Sacrament of his body, and wine as a Sacrament of his blood, to testify by them unto us, that, as certainly as we receive and hold this Sacrament in our hands, and eat and drink the same with our mouths, by which our life is afterwards nourished, we also do as certainly receive by faith (which is the hand and mouth of our soul) the true body and blood of Christ our only Saviour in our souls, for the support of our spiritual life.

Now, as it is certain and beyond all doubt that Jesus Christ hath not enjoined to us the use of his Sacraments in vain, so he works in us all that he represents to us by these holy signs, though the manner surpasses our understanding, and can not be comprehended by us, as the operations of the Holy Ghost are hidden and incomprehensible. In the mean time we err not when we say that what is eaten and drunk by us is the proper and natural body and the proper blood of Christ. But the manner of our partaking of the same is not by the mouth, but by the Spirit through faith. Thus, then, though Christ always sits at the right hand of his Father in the heavens, yet doth he not, therefore, cease to make us partakers of himself by faith. This feast is a spiritual table, at which Christ communicates himself with all his benefits to us, and gives us there to enjoy both himself and the merits of his sufferings and death, nourishing, strengthening, and comforting our poor comfortless souls, by the eating of his flesh, quickening and refreshing them by the drinking of his blood.

This is certainly a compact theology, but those who sing the communion hymns of Charles Wesley, the great Methodist, will have met the same doctrine there.

The Council of Trent rejected virtually all the Protestant criticisms and set forth the essence of the medieval doctrines in its *Decree concerning the most Holy Sacrament of the Eucharist* of 11 October 1551 and in its *Doctrine of the Sacrifice of the Mass* of 17 September 1562. The first of these contained these three canons:

CANON I. — If any one denieth, that, in the sacrament of the most holy Eucharist, are contained truly, really, and substantially, the body and blood together with the soul and divinity of our Lord Jesus Christ, and consequently the whole Christ; but said that he is only therein as in a sign, or in figure, or virtue: let him be anathema.

CANON II. — If any one saith, that, in the sacred and holy sacrament of the Eucharist, the substance of the bread and wine remains conjointly with the body and blood of our Lord Jesus Christ, and denieth that wonderful and singular conversion of the whole substance of the bread into the body, and of the whole substance of the wine into the blood — the species only of the bread and wine remaining — which conversion indeed the Catholic Church most aptly calls Transubstantiation: let him be anathema.

CANON III. — If any one denieth, that, in the venerable sacrament of the Eucharist, the whole Christ is contained under each species, and under every part of each species, when separated: let him be anathema.

Here is transubstantiation and the defence of communion

in one kind.

The second document confirmed that 'in this divine sacrifice which is celebrated in the Mass, the same Christ is contained and immolated in an unbloody manner who once offered himself in a bloody manner on the altar of the Cross'. Thus 'the sacrifice is truly propitiatory' and the 'victim is one and the same, the same now offering by the ministry of the priests, who then offered himself on the Cross, the manner alone of offering being different'. Then it summarised the matter in these three canons:

CANON I. — If any one saith, that in the mass a true and proper sacrifice is not offered to God; or, that to be offered is nothing else but that Christ is given us to eat: let him be anathema.

CANON II. — If any one saith, that by those words, *Do this for the commemoration of me* (Luke xxii. 19), Christ did not institute the apostles priests; or, did not ordain that they and other priests should offer his own body and blood: let him be anathema.

CANON III. — If any one saith. that the sacrifice of the mass is only a sacrifice of praise and of thanksgiving; or, that it is a bare commemoration of the sacrifice consummated on the cross, but not a propitiatory sacrifice; or, that it profits him only who receives; and that it ought not to be offered for the living and the dead for sins, pains, satisfactions, and other necessities: let him be anathema.

The Protestants were so convinced that the sacrifice of Christ took place once, for all, in space and time, that they could not conceive of any repetition of it, only the remembrance of it in the presence of the Christ who had died but was alive for evermore.

Protestants, however, were conscious of sacrificial themes within the Eucharist. There was the commemoration of the one sacrifice of Christ: 'Almighty God, our heavenly Father who of thy tender mercy didst give thine only Son, Jesus Christ, to suffer death on the cross for our redemption; who made there (by his one oblation of himself once offered) a full, perfect, and sufficient sacrifice, oblation, and satisfaction for the sins of the whole world. . .' (Prayer of Consecration, *Book of Common Prayer*). There was the sacrifice of praise and thanksgiving; 'O Lord and heavenly Father, we thy humble servants entirely desire thy fatherly goodness mercifully to accept this our sacrifice of praise and thanksgiving. . .' This same prayer goes on to state the other idea of sacrifice: 'Here we offer and present unto thee, O Lord, ourselves, our souls and bodies, to be a reasonable, holy and lively sacrifice unto thee. . .' (Prayer after Communion, *Book of Common Prayer*). Roman Catholics readily accepted the themes of sacrifices of thanksgiving and of ourselves. The great difference is in the way in which the one sacrifice of Christ, a historical event with eternal effects, is commemorated. Roman Catholics affirmed (in a sophisticated way), and Protestants denied, that there was a repetition of the one sacrifice of Christ.

It would be wrong to assume that the Roman Catholic doctrine of the Eucharist has remained static since the Council of Trent. Without denying any of the doctrines set forth at the Council of Trent, the Second Vatican Council placed them in a richer context and stated the very controversial areas with great care and sensitivity. It is generally recognised that one of the achievements of this modern council was to emphasise and express the close relationship between the 'mystery' of the Church and the 'mystery' of the Eucharist. The celebration of the latter is seen as the outstanding means whereby the faithful can express in their lives and manifest to others the 'mystery' of Christ and the real nature of the true Church.

Although references to the Eucharist occur in various documents it is in *Instruction on the Worship of the Eucharistic Mystery* (1967) that a clear summary is given by the Vatican Sacred Congregation of Rites of the principal points of the doctrine of the Eucharist. After referring to recent documents [e.g. the *Dogmatic Constitution on the Church* of Vatican II, and two Encyclicals, *Mediator Dei* (1947)] and *Mysterium Fidei* (1965) this chapter states:

Among the doctrinal principles concerning the Eucharist formulated in these documents of the Church, the following should be noted as having a bearing upon the attitude of Christians towards this mystery, and, therefore, as falling within the scope of this Instruction.

a. 'The Son of God in the human nature which he united to himself redeemed man and transformed him into a new creation by overcoming death through his own death and resurrection (cf. Gal. 6:15; 2 Cor. 5:17). For by giving his spirit he mystically established as his body his brethren gathered from all nations. In that body the life of Christ is communicated to those who believe; for through the sacraments they are joined in a mysterious yet real way to the Christ who suffered and is glorified.'

Therefore 'Our Saviour at the Last Supper on the night when he was betrayed instituted the eucharistic sacrifices of his Body and Blood so that he might perpetuate the sacrifice of the cross throughout the centuries till his coming. He thus entrusted to the Church, his beloved spouse, a memorial of his death and resurrection: a sacrament of love, a sign of unity, a bond of charity, a paschal meal in which Christ is eaten, the mind filled with grace and a pledge of future glory given to us.'

Hence the Mass, the Lord's Supper, is at the same time and inseparably:

a sacrifice in which the sacrifice of the cross is perpetuated;

a memorial of the death and resurrection of the Lord, who said 'do this in memory of me' (Luke 22:19);

a sacred banquet in which, through the communion

of the Body and Blood of the Lord, the People of God share the benefits of the Paschal Sacrifice, renew the New Covenant which God has made with man once for all through the Blood of Christ, and in faith and hope foreshadow and anticipate the eschatological banquet in the kingdom of the Father, proclaiming the Lord's death 'till his coming'.

b. In the Mass, therefore, the sacrifice and sacred meal belong to the same mystery — so much so that they are linked by the closest bond.

For in the sacrifice of the Mass Our Lord is immolated when 'he begins to be present sacramentally as the spiritual food of the faithful under the appearances of bread and wine'. It was for this purpose that Christ entrusted this sacrifice to the Church, that the faithful might share in it both spiritually, by faith and charity, and sacramentally, through the banquet of Holy Communion. Participation in the Lord's Supper is always communion with Christ offering himself for us as a sacrifiice to the Father.

c. The celebration of the Eucharist which takes place at Mass is the action not only of Christ, but also of the Church. For in it Christ perpetuates in an unbloody manner the sacrifice offered on the cross, offering himself to the Father for the world's salvation through the ministry of priests. The Church, the spouse and minister of Christ, performs together with him the role of priest and victim, offers him to the Father and at the same time makes a total offering of herself together with him.

Thus, the Church, especially in the great Eucharistic Prayer, together with Christ, gives thanks to the Father in the Holy Spirit for all the blessings which he gives to men in creation and especially in the Paschal Mystery, and prays to him for the coming of his kingdom.

d. Hence no Mass, indeed no liturgical action, is a purely private action, but rather a celebration of the

Church as a society composed of different orders and ministries in which each member acts according to his own order and role.

e. The celebration of the Eucharist in the sacrifice of the Mass is the origin and consummation of the worship shown to the Eucharist outside Mass. Not only are the sacred species which remain after the Mass derived from the Mass, but they are preserved so that those of the faithful who cannot come to Mass may be united to Christ, and his sacrifice celebrated in the Mass, through sacramental communion received with the right dispositions.

Consequently the eucharistic sacrifice is the source and the summit of the whole of the Church's worship and of the Christian life. The faithful participate more fully in this sacrament of thanksgiving, propitiation, petition and praise, not only when they whole-heartedly offer the sacred victim, and in it themselves, to the Father with the priest, but also when they receive this same victim sacramentally.

f. There should be no doubt in anyone's mind 'that all the faithful ought to show to this most holy sacrament the worship which is due to the true God, as has always been the custom of the Catholic Church. Nor is it to be adored any the less because it was instituted by Christ to be eaten.' For even in the reserved sacrament he is to be adored because he is substantially present there through that conversion of bread and wine which, as the Council of Trent tells us, is most aptly named transubstantiation.

g. The mystery of the Eucharist should therefore be considered in all its fullness, not only in the celebration of Mass but also in devotion to the sacred species which remain after Mass and are reserved to extend the grace of the sacrifice.

These are the principles from which practical rules are to be drawn to govern devotion due to the sacrament outside Mass and its proper relation to the right ordering of the sacrifice of the Mass according to the mind of the Second Vatican Council and the other documents of the Apostolic See on this subject.

The idea of the Mass as a sacrifice offered to God remains; but the language is more restrained than in previous conciliar and papal pronouncements. And the prominent idea of the offering of Christ is skilfully integrated with other (Protestants would say) biblical ideas of sacrifice — e.g. of the whole congregation offering itself as a sacrifice to God. Further, although the term 'transubstantiation' is not used, there is here a full doctrine of the real presence of Christ in the consecrated elements. This is the basis for the practice of adoration of Christ in the reserved sacrament.

While it is true that private Masses are not as common as they were, that Holy Communion is often given in both kinds to the laity, that there is little talk of 'propitiatory sacrifice' or 'transubstantiation', that the vernacular is everywhere now used, and that there is much more emphasis on the Eucharist as the celebration of all God's people, it is also true that Roman Catholic doctrine in this area has not fundamentally changed.

It is possible, however, that with greater understanding of what *anamnesis* ('remembrance') meant, in ancient Israel and for the writers of the New Testament, there will develop greater possibilities for some common mind on the relation of the one sacrifice of Christ in history to the eucharistic 'sacrifice' in the Church. And, greater knowledge of the understanding of Christ's presence in this sacrament as taught by the early Church, may also help to bridge the gap in this area.

8: Does Mary really help?

Protestants are often puzzled, and are sometimes annoyed, by the fact that Roman Catholics venerate and invoke the saints. Roman Catholics, for their part, are continually amazed that Protestants should have such negative views of the Blessed Virgin Mary and all the saints. There is little said on the subject by Protestants, either positively or negatively, in their confessions of faith; while Roman Catholics have inherited from the mediaeval Church (and have subsequently developed) a rich theology and practice in this area.

Background

The veneration of the saints and of Mary as the Blessed Virgin Mother of God gained momentum and depth as the Church lived and worshipped in the Roman Empire. The general theology underlying the practice has two emphases. Firstly, the saints are close to God because of their holiness. Secondly, as human beings they are also close to, and identified with, all humanity. Hence they are able to intercede for the faithful on earth or in Purgatory (the place or sphere where Christians are further sanctified and purified, between earth and heaven). The veneration and invocation of the saints was not a peripheral part of the faith of the Church. It formed part of the liturgy for the Eucharist every Sunday.

To venerate the saints (or their ikons — their images) might seem to be robbing God of the worship due to him as Lord, and the problem was recognised. The Second Council of Nicea (787) clearly distinguished between veneration due to the saints (Greek *doulia*, Latin *dulia* and *veneratio*), and genuine worship (Greek *latreia*, Latin

107

latria and *adoratio*) due only to God himself. It became the practice, because Mary was regarded as being in a class by herself, to refer to veneration of Mary as '*hyperdulia*' (from the Greek *huper-doulia*, 'more than veneration'), but such veneration is still not the same as true worship of God.

These distinctions became firmly embedded in the theology of the mediaeval Western Church. However, the careful distinctions made by the theologians were not always reflected in the practice of the faithful. Popular devotion, in various ways, took on the nature of a cult, paying scant attention to official theology. Instead of a particular saint being regarded as a witness to the gospel and a model of holiness for others to follow, he or she was seen as a 'supernatural friend', who helped to overcome the many problems and difficulties of life. Far from veneration being restrained and controlled, the impulse was to worship the saint. Images and relics of saints were given divine status, and pilgrimages to shrines multiplied and became a feature of popular mediaeval religion.

The protest of the reformers

The reformers wanted to uphold the centrality of Jesus Christ as the only mediator and heavenly intercessor. Also, they wanted to do justice to the meaning of the word 'saint' as the New Testament used it. So they were forced to attack much popular — and with it, some official — teaching and practice concerning the veneration and invocation of Mary and the saints.

In the *Ten Theses of Berne* (1528), there is a brief but telling statement: 'As Christ alone died for us, so he is to be worshipped as the only Mediator and Advocate between God the Father and us believers. Therefore, to propose the invoking of other mediators and advocates beyond this life is contrary to Scripture.' It is a theme which is enlarged in the *Geneva Confession* (1536):

12. Invocation of God only and intercession of Christ

As we have declared that we have confidence and hope for salvation and all good only in God through Jesus Christ, so we confess that we ought to invoke him in all necessities in the name of Jesus Christ, who is our Mediator and Advocate with him and has access to him. Likewise we ought to acknowledge that all good things come from him alone, and to give thanks to him for them. On the other hand, we reject the intercession of the saints as a superstition invented by men contrary to Scripture, for the reason that it proceeds from mistrust of the sufficiency of the intercession of Jesus Christ.

Here we see the great Protestant emphasis on 'Christ alone' emerging.

Meanwhile the *Augsburg Confession* (1530) represented the teaching of the German Lutherans on the matter:

XXI. — Of the Worship of Saints Touching the worship of saints, they teach that the memory of saints may be set before us, that we may follow their faith and good works according to our calling; as the Emperor may follow David's example in making war to drive away the Turks from his country; for either of them is a king. But the Scripture teacheth not to invocate saints, or to ask help of saints, because it propoundeth unto us one Christ the Mediator, Propitiatory, High-Priest, and Intercessor. This Christ is to be invocated, and he hath promised that he will hear our prayers, and liketh this worship especially, to wit, that he be invocated in all afflictions. 'If any man sin, we have an advocate with God, Jesus Christ the righteous' (1 John ii. 1).

Here there is a positive evaluation, both of 'Christ alone' and of the saints.

After the Council of Trent had confirmed the traditional teaching, the *Second Helvetic Confession* (1566) reaffirmed the principle that God is to be invoked only through the mediation of Christ, the heavenly High Priest (Chapter 5). Then it continued:

The Saints Are Not to Be Adored, Worshipped or Invoked For this reason we do not adore, worship, or pray to the saints in heaven, or to other gods, and we do not acknowledge them as our intercessors or mediators before the Father in heaven. For God and Christ the Mediator are sufficient for us; neither do we give to others the honour that is due to God alone and to his Son, because he has expressly said: 'My glory I give to no other' (Isa. 42:8), and because Peter has said: "There is no other name under heaven given among men by which we must be saved," except the name of Christ (Acts 4:12). In him, those who give their assent by faith do not seek anything outside Christ.

The Due Honour to Be Rendered to the Saints At the same time we do not despise the saints or think basely of them. For we acknowledge them to be living members of Christ and friends of God who have gloriously overcome the flesh and the world. Hence we love them as brothers, and also honour them; yet not with any kind of worship but by an honourable opinion of them and just praise of them. We also imitate them. For with ardent longings and supplications we earnestly desire to be imitators of their faith and virtues, to share eternal salvation with them, to dwell eternally with them in the presence of God, and to rejoice with them in Christ. And in this respect we approve of the opinion of St. Augustine in *De Vera Religione:* 'Let not our religion be the cult of men who have died. For if they have lived holy lives, they are not to be thought of as seeking such honours; on the contrary, they want us to worship him by whose illumination they rejoice that we are fellow-servants of his merits. They are therefore to be honoured by way of imitation, but not to be adored in a religious manner,' etc.

Relics of the Saints Much less do we believe that the relics of the saints are to be adored and reverenced. Those ancient saints seemed to have sufficiently honoured their dead when they decently committed their remains to the earth after the spirit had ascended on high. And they thought that the most noble relics of their ancestors were their virtues, their doctrine, and their faith. Moreover, as they commend these 'relics' when praising the dead, so they strive to copy them during their life on earth.

Here we note again the denial of certain Roman Catholic doctrines, coupled with a positive affirmation regarding the example that the saints provide.

From Trent to Vatican II

As part of the *Decree concerning Purgatory* (1563) the Council of Trent reaffirmed the Church's commitment to the invocation and veneration of the saints and their relics. And it required of all bishops, priests and teachers:

. . . to instruct the faithful diligently, in particular as regards the intercession and the invocation of the saints, the honour due to their relics, and the lawful use of images. Let them teach the faithful that the saints, reigning together with Christ, pray to God for men; that it is good and useful to invoke them humbly and to have recourse to their prayers, to their help and assistance, in order to obtain favours from God through His Son, our Lord Jesus Christ who alone is our Redeemer and Saviour. Those who deny that the saints enjoying eternal happiness in heaven are to be invoked; or who claim that saints do not pray for men or that calling upon them to pray for each of us is idolatry or is opposed to the word of God and is prejudicial to the honour of Jesus Christ, the one Mediator between God and men (*cf. 1 Tim. 2.5*); or who say that it is foolish to make supplication orally or mentally to those who are reigning in heaven; all those entertain impious thoughts.

Thus the cult of Mary and the cult of the saints became a prominent feature of Roman Catholic worship and devotion.

Because the doctrine of Mary has undergone development whereas the doctrine of the saints has not, we shall concentrate on Mariology. (There is an important distinction between 'Mariology', which means the doctrines concerning Mary, and 'Mariolatry', which means the worship of Mary. The latter has never been officially commended by Roman Catholics, but some Protestants have accused Roman Catholics of practising it.)

Perhaps the easiest way to think of the development of Mariology is that there were three stages. With the first of these Protestants agree, and it is found in the teaching of the Councils of Ephesus (431) and of Chalcedon (451). Mary was described as *theotokos* ('God-bearer', or 'mother of God'), in order to preserve the greater truth that Jesus Christ her son is truly God made man, the Word made flesh. Originally the title *'theotokos'* was given in order to honour Christ and direct a proper doctrine and worship of him.

Once what may be called the 'divine motherhood' of Mary had been established, the way was opened up (and followed) towards a greater understanding and clarification of its implications for Mary herself, in terms of the special vocation she had received from God. This has historically led to the doctrines of Mary's sinlessness, her immaculate conception, and her bodily assumption into heaven. These doctrines only became official dogma, to be believed by all the faithful, in modern times.

Finally, her personal vocation having been established, Mary's role within the people of God and in the mystery of salvation had to be made clear; in this connection Vatican II made a particular contribution.

The development of the dogma of Mary's personal vocation can be said to have begun with the papal bull *Ineffabilis Deus* of 8 December 1854. This set forth, as a dogma of the Church, the doctrine known as the Immaculate Conception of the Blessed Virgin Mary. The doctrine was not new, only the fact that belief in it was now obligatory upon the faithful. The heart of the statement reads:

> To the glory of the holy and undivided Trinity, to the honour and renown of the Virgin Mother of God, the exaltation of the Catholic faith and the increase of Christian religion; by the authority of our Lord Jesus Christ, of the blessed apostles Peter and Paul, and by our own authority, we declare, pronounce and define: the doctrine which holds that the most Blessed Virgin Mary was, from the first moment of her conception, by the singular grace and privilege of almighty God and in view of the merits of Christ Jesus the Saviour of the human race, preserved immune from all stain of original sin, is revealed by God and, therefore, firmly and constantly to be believed by all the faithful.
> If, therefore, any persons shall dare to think — which God forbid — otherwise than has been defined by us, let them clearly know that they stand condemned by their own judgment, that they have made shipwreck of their faith and fallen from the unity of the Church. Furthermore, they subject themselves *ipso facto* to the penalties provided by law if by speech or writing or in any other exterior way they shall dare to express their views.

There was no attempt to justify it on scriptural grounds. It was simply taken out of the developing tradition of the Church and elevated into a dogma. The day on which the bull was promulgated — 8 December — is celebrated annually as the Feast of the Immaculate Conception.

Almost a century later came another papal declaration of a new dogma concerning Mary: that, having completed her life on earth, she died and was taken up body and soul into heaven from the grave. On 1 November 1950 Pope Pius XII defined the doctrine of the Assumption of the Blessed Virgin Mary as a dogma of the Church, binding on all the faithful. His Apostolic Constitution, *Munificentissimus Deus*, offered a survey of the belief in this doctrine and then defined it as follows:

From all eternity and by one and the same decree of predestination the august Mother of God is united in a sublime way with Jesus Christ; immaculate in her conception, a spotless virgin in her divine mother-hood, the noble companion of the divine Redeemer who won a complete triumph over sin and its consequences, she finally obtained as the crowning glory of her privileges to be preserved from the corruption of the tomb and, like her Son before her, to conquer death and to be raised body and soul to the glory of heaven, to shine refulgent as Queen at the right hand of her Son, the immortal King of ages (*cf. 1 Tim. 1.17*).

The universal Church, in which the Spirit of truth actively dwells, and which is infallibly guided by Him to an ever more perfect knowledge of revealed truths, has down the centuries manifested her belief in many ways; the bishops from all over the world ask almost unanimously that the truth of the bodily Assumption of the Blessed Virgin Mary into heaven be defined as a dogma of divine and catholic faith; this truth is based on Sacred Scripture and deeply embedded in the minds of the faithful; it has received the approval of liturgical worship from the earliest times; it is perfectly in keeping with the rest of revealed truth, and has been lucidly developed and explained by the studies, the knowledge and wisdom of theologians. Considering all these reasons we deem that the moment pre-ordained in the plan of divine providence has now arrived for us to proclaim solemnly this extraordinary privilege of the

Virgin Mary. . . .

Therefore, having directed humble and repeated prayers to God, and having invoked the light of the Spirit of Truth; to the glory of almighty God who has bestowed His special bounty on the Virgin Mary, for the honour of His Son the immortal King of ages and victor over sin and death, for the greater glory of His august mother, and for the joy and exultation of the whole Church; by the authority of our Lord Jesus Christ, of the blessed apostles Peter and Paul, and by our own authority, we proclaim, declare and define as a dogma revealed by God: the Immaculate Mother of God, Mary ever Virgin, when the course of her earthly life was finished, was taken up body and soul into the glory of heaven.

Wherefore, if anyone — which God forbid — should wilfully dare to deny or call in doubt what has been defined by us, let him know that he certainly has abandoned the divine and catholic faith.

Perhaps the most important question that Protestants have raised about this statement is simply, 'Where is the scriptural evidence for this doctrine?'

After the promulgation of the dogma of the Assumption, Marian devotion in the Roman Church was at a high level. It has generally remained so. Each year over two million people visit the shrine of our Lady at Lourdes, and a thousand or more books about her are published each year. Understandably, at the Second Vatican Council there was great pressure to produce a separate document or decree on Mary, and to make her role as Mediatrix clear (mediator of grace through her intercession before our Lord). This proposal was narrowly defeated. Instead, the teaching on Mary appeared in the *Dogmatic Constitution on the Church* (1964), of which chapter 8 is entitled 'The Blessed Virgin Mary, Mother of God in the Mystery of Christ and the Church'.

The chapter's preface states that Mary 'is hailed as

preeminent and as a wholly unique member of our Church, and as its type and outstanding model in faith and charity'. It is a sophisticated chapter, written in such a way as to anchor Mary's role firmly in the biblical material about her in the Gospels. In addition, it is asserted that whatever is true of Mary's role in no way detracts from that of Christ.

In a humble yet significant way Mary played her part in the mystery of salvation by freely consenting to the role of divine motherhood. In a real sense, God was dependent upon her.

The Father of mercies willed that the Incarnation should be preceeded by assent on the part of the predestined mother, so that just as a woman had a share in bringing about death, so also a woman should contribute to life. This is preeminently true of the Mother of Jesus, who gave to the world the Life that renews all things, and who was enriched by God with gifts appropriate to such a role. It is no wonder then that it was customary for the Fathers to refer to the Mother of God as all holy and free from every stain of sin, as though fashioned by the Holy Spirit and formed as a new creature. Enriched from the first instant of her conception with the splendor of an entirely unique holiness, the virgin of Nazareth is hailed by the heralding angel, by divine command, as 'full of grace' (cf. Luke 1:28) and to the heavenly messenger she replies: 'Behold the handmaid of the Lord, be it done unto me according to thy word' (Luke 1:38). Thus the daughter of Adam, Mary, consenting to the word of God, became the Mother of Jesus. Committing herself whole-heartedly and impeded by no sin to God's saving will, she devoted herself totally, as a handmaid of the Lord, to the person and work of her Son, under and with him, serving the mystery of redemption, by the grace of Almighty God. Rightly, therefore, the Fathers see Mary not merely as passively engaged by God, but as freely cooperating in the work of man's

116

salvation through faith and obedience. For, as St Irenaeus says, she 'being obedient, became the cause of salvation for herself and for the whole human race.'

And, since she is (in Irenaeus' words) 'the cause of salvation', she must also be intimately related to the Church of God, bought with the blood of her son:

The predestination of the Blessed Virgin as Mother of God was associated with the incarnation of the divine word: in the designs of divine Providence she was the gracious mother of the divine Redeemer here on earth, and above all others and in a singular way the generous associate and humble handmaid of the Lord. She conceived, brought forth, and nourished Christ, she presented him to the Father in the temple, shared her Son's sufferings as he died on the cross. Thus, in a wholly singular way she cooperated by her obedience, faith, hope and burning charity in the work of the Saviour in restoring supernatural life to souls. For this reason she is a mother to us in the order of grace.

This motherhood of Mary in the order of grace continues uninterruptedly from the consent which she loyally gave at the Annunciation and which she sustained without wavering beneath the cross, until the eternal fulfilment of all the elect. Taken up to heaven she did not lay aside this saving office but by her manifold intercession continues to bring us the gifts of eternal salvation. By her maternal charity, she cares for the brethren of her Son, who still journey on earth surrounded by dangers and difficulties, until they are led into their blessed home. Therefore the Blessed Virgin is invoked in the Church under the titles of Advocate, Helper, Benefactress, and Mediatrix. This, however, is so understood that it neither takes away anything from nor adds anything to the dignity and efficacy of Christ the one Mediator.

Here Mary is called 'Mediatrix'. Including this title made a number of members of the Council unhappy, because they feared Protestants would misunderstand and think that Mary was being described as in a sense Christ's equal. The title was left in, because of its frequent usage by recent Popes. However, the impact was softened by putting alongside it other, less controversial titles, and by following it with the assertion that there is only one Mediator between God and mankind: Jesus Christ.

Thus the common criticism, often voiced in Protestant circles and indeed rooted in the original protest of the Reformation itself, is still heard — that Marian doctrines and piety tend to put a barrier between Christ and believers. Most Protestant theologians admire the edifice of Marian doctrine and think they understand its logic, but the Protestant Churches in general have shown few signs of moving towards this Marian doctrine and piety. Ecumenical teams have gone a long way towards building a common understanding of the biblical and patristic evidence concerning Mary, but the development of the doctrine since the Reformation has left most Protestants far behind. Here is still a major area of disagreement.

Epilogue

The question we set out to ask was, 'What is the difference?'. The answer that emerges is that so far as the official teaching of Roman Catholics and Protestants is concerned, there are several major and many minor differences.

Perhaps the most significant difference is the fact that the Roman Catholic Church cannot exist without the Magisterium. There could be no Church, no gospel, no sacraments and no teaching without the Pope and the college of bishops. In the final analysis, Roman Catholic Christianity cannot even exist as a phenomenon within human history without the historic order of bishops with the Pope as its head. In contrast, Protestantism can exist as a form of Christianity wherever a group of believers in Jesus Christ meet together. In the end, what matters is the invisible but direct relationship of Christ to his believing people. Grace is free. It does not depend on a ministerial hierarchy.

If there is any truth in these comments then a profound difference of approach to Christianity lies at the heart of the differences between classic Roman Catholicism and classic Protestantism. A perceptive biblical scholar, F.J. Leenhardt of Geneva, charitably portrayed the two approaches in a book published two decades ago: *Two biblical faiths: Protestant and Catholic* (1964). He saw the two faiths as heirs to two types of spirituality; the Abrahamic and the Mosaic.

Leenhardt described Abrahamic spirituality as that in which man is addressed directly by the Word of God who speaks to the heart. It is this which Protestantism inherits, for it ultimately concerns a personal relationship with God and a personal response to him expressed by doing his will. Protestant piety is essentially interior and personal, listening to and responding to the pure word of God; it wants to give the Holy Spirit room to move. So, while the fellowship of believers is very important, Abrahamic spirituality suspects the authority of human traditions. It opposes placing anybody, even that lovely lady Mary the mother of Jesus, between earth and the Saviour in heaven. It wants direct access to the throne of grace. It has no wish to be encumbered with a complex sacramental system. Abrahamic spirituality is personal but not individualist. It desires fellowship, but not domination.

Protestant spirituality is in essence simple. Roman Catholic spirituality is in essence complex; this is one reason why it may be called an heir of Mosaic spirituality. Leenhardt wrote:

> With Moses. . . . . Revelation entered into the continuity of history, it became interwoven with the life of the world, assuming concrete forms. Absolute in its essence, which of course it remains, it now becomes relative in its manifestations, it becomes contingent, mixed, disputable. Whereas the word of God committed Abraham to a way which involved him in a decisive break, depriving him of all 'worldly' support, and compelling him to walk ahead as seeing nothing, his attention absorbed by the eschatological promise, the word of God disclosed itself to Moses in the shape of sensuously apprehensible phenomena, in visible and audible signs, and to that extent it entered into composition with and was compromised by that which was not authentically itself. The revelation to Moses inaugurated a delicate dialectic of nature and grace. (p. 93)

Roman Catholic spirituality as it has developed over the centuries, argues Leenhardt, may be said to revolve around two axes. One is the historical embodiment of Revelation in the Church, the 'Body of Christ', understood as a prolonging or extending of the incarnation of the Son of God, Jesus Christ. The other is the transcendent order of grace, invisible but nonetheless real, communicated to the faithful through the ministrations of the divinely-appointed order of priests as they celebrate and administer the seven sacraments, chiefly the Eucharist.

It is worth pondering what Leenhardt wrote. For me, it raises some interesting questions. Is there one single New Testament spirituality, for which everybody should search? Or are there several New Testament spiritualities, all equally valuable, all equally valid — and all transcending the 'Abrahamic' and 'Mosaic' types of spirituality? Further: what about the early Church? How did spirituality express itself, and what relationship did it have to the spirituality of the apostolic period? These and other questions call for answers!

In the belief that true good would come to the world if Roman Catholicism and Protestantism could grow towards each other, I want to make the following suggestions. I make them on the basis of certain convictions: that the lines of the separate and opposing theologies are so well drawn that an attempt has to be made by both sides to find a new way of doing theology; and that only when people live together, and interact as people, is there any true possibility of growth in understanding and a possibility for change.

In every region, large or small (depending on interest and need) there is need for a group of 'educated' Roman Catholics and Protestants to live, worship and work together for several months or more at one time. As they come to know each other, to respect each other's personality with its strengths and weaknesses, and to enjoy common worship together, they will regularly and carefully study the Bible and seek to agree on what it means. The intention would be, rather than immediately to jump to how the Church or parts of the Church has understood the Bible, to use all available helps —

dictionaries and so on — to find out what the original authors intended, and what that intention could or should mean for Christians today. The study would be undertaken in an atmosphere of prayer and worship.

These small, committed groups should be seen as front-runners in a race in which all Christians are involved in their own part of the world. In each parish, attempts would be made to discover as many ways as possible of having Roman Catholics and Protestants make contact, be it in practical activity or acts of worship, prayer or study. Then, from time to time, the members of the 'intense' group could visit the parochial groups and report on how they were learning to think new thoughts, to evaluate the Christian faith afresh, to see Christ in their fellows, and so on. Membership of the committed groups could change periodically so that those with the new vision could return to the local scene to encourage Christians there. Hopefully, over several years this process would contribute to the genuine search for truth and unity, and would actually gain in momentum. Attempts at mutual understanding have in recent years been too closely connected with central committees, commissions and the like. As a result, many people have become tired of talk of 'ecumenism'. It has been a reality too far removed from their experience.

In the long term, the work of denominational, national or international commissions seeking to propose 'agreement' on this or that doctrine will be useless — unless there is a movement from the grass roots. Indeed, if there were to be a genuine cry from the parishes and congregations for moves towards greater understanding and fellowship, the theologians' work would be much easier, and more relevant. Such a new initiative would create the context in which a new way could be found of doing, and presenting, theology.

I have made these basic suggestions — which would apply in the majority of western countries — but I realise that there are many problems involved. For example,

Protestants are not agreed among themselves. But what I suggest could have a reconciling and healing effect on Protestant divisions. Then there is the fact that Roman Catholicism is to a large extent controlled from the Vatican City in Rome. Since Italy, like Spain and Portugal, is a Roman Catholic country, it is unlikely that what could happen in terms of mutual understanding in Holland, Germany, Britain and America could happen in the same way in Italy. Nevertheless there is no reason why winds of change should not blow from America, Northern Europe and the developing world — into the Vatican City. If it is God's wind it will blow where our sovereign Lord decrees that it should blow. We certainly need God's wind.

I am primarily addressing Protestants. Let me end by reminding them of the famous statement: *Ecclesia reformata sed semper reformanda* ('The church, reformed but always to be reformed'). The Reformation is not complete. God has still more truth to illuminate in the sacred Scriptures, and Christ calls us all to more careful listening and more committed obedience to that truth. In the dialogue with Roman Catholics, and in the mutual study of the Bible, God may well continue his work of reformation.

Appendix 1:
Three Catholic Creeds

A: The Apostles' Creed

I believe in God, the Father almighty,
creator of heaven and earth.

I believe in Jesus Christ, his only Son,
  our Lord.
He was conceived by the power of the
  Holy Spirit
and born of the Virgin Mary.
He suffered under Pontius Pilate,
was crucified, died, and was buried.
He descended to the dead.
On the third day he rose again.
He ascended into heaven,
and is seated at the right hand
  of the Father.
He will come again to judge the living
  and the dead.

I believe in the Holy Spirit,
the holy catholic Church,
the communion of saints,
the forgiveness of sins,
the resurrection of the body,
and the life everlasting. Amen.

B: The Nicene Creed

We believe in one God,
  the Father, the almighty,

maker of heaven and earth,
of all that is,
seen and unseen.

We believe in one Lord, Jesus Christ,
the only Son of God,
eternally begotten of the Father,
God from God, Light from Light,
true God from true God,
begotten, not made,
of one Being with the Father.
Through him all things were made.
For us men and for our salvation
he came down from heaven;
by the power of the Holy Spirit
he became incarnate of the Virgin Mary,
    and was made man.
For our sake he was crucified under
    Pontius Pilate;
he suffered death and was buried.
On the third day he rose again
in accordance with the Scriptures;
he ascended into heaven
and is seated at the right hand of the Father.
He will come again in glory
to judge the living and the dead,
and his kingdom will have no end.

We believe in the Holy Spirit,
the Lord, the giver of life,
who proceeds from the Father [and the Son].
With the Father and the Son he is worshipped
    and glorified.
He has spoken through the Prophets.

We believe in one holy catholic
    and apostolic Church.
We acknowledge one baptism for the
    forgiveness of sins.
We look for the resurrection of the dead,
and the life of the world to come. Amen.

C: The Athanasian Creed

Whosoever wishes to be saved
before all things it is necessary that he hold the catholic
   faith,
which faith, if anyone does not keep it whole and
   unharmed,
without doubt he will perish everlastingly.
Now, the catholic faith is this,
that we worship one God in Trinity, and Trinity in
   Unity,
neither confusing the Persons
nor dividing the divine Being.
For there is one Person of the Father, another of the
   Son,
and another of the Holy Spirit,
but the Godhead of the Father, the Son and the Holy
   Spirit is all one,
their glory equal, their majesty co-eternal.
Such as the Father is, such is the Son
and such is the Holy Spirit:
the Father uncreated, the Son uncreated
and the Holy Spirit uncreated,
the Father infinite, the Son infinite
and the Holy Spirit infinite,
the Father eternal, the Son eternal
and the Holy Spirit eternal;
and yet they are not three Eternals
but one Eternal,
just as they are not three Uncreateds, nor three
   Infinites,
but one Uncreated and one Infinite.
In the same way, the Father is almighty, the Son
   almighty
and the Holy Spirit almighty,
and yet they are not three Almighties
but one Almighty.
Thus, the Father is God, the Son is God
and the Holy Spirit is God,

and yet there are not three Gods
but one God.
Thus, the Father is the Lord, the Son is the Lord,
and the Holy Spirit is God,
and yet not three Lords
but one Lord.
Because, just as we are compelled by Christian truth
to confess each Person singly to be both God and Lord,
so are we forbidden by the catholic religion
to say, There are three Gods, or three Lords.
The Father is from none,
not made nor created, nor begotten;
the Son is from the Father alone,
not made nor created, but begotten;
the Holy Spirit is from the Father and the Son,
not made nor created nor begotten, but proceeding.
So there is one Father, not three Fathers; one Son,
    not three Sons;
one Holy Spirit, not three Holy Spirits.
And in this Trinity there is no before or after,
no greater or less,
but all three Persons are co-eternal with each other
and co-equal.
So that in all things, as has already been said,
the Trinity in Unity, and Unity in Trinity, is to be
    worshipped.
He therefore who wishes to be saved
let him think thus of the Trinity.
Furthermore, it is necessary to everlasting salvation
that he should faithfully believe the incarnation of our
    Lord Jesus Christ.
Now, the right faith is that we should believe and
    confess
that our Lord Jesus Christ, the Son of God, is both
    God and man equally.
He is God from the Being of the Father, begotten
    before the worlds,
and he is man from the being of his mother, born in
    the world;

perfect God and perfect man,
having both man's rational soul and human flesh;
equal to the Father as regards his divinity
and inferior to the Father as regards his humanity;
who, although he is God and man,
yet he is not two, but one Christ;
one, however, not by the conversion of the Godhead
into flesh
but by the taking up of the humanity into God;
utterly one, not by confusion of human and divine
being
but by unity of Christ's one Person.
For just as the rational soul and the flesh are one man,
so God and man are one Christ;
who suffered for our salvation,
descended to Sheol, rose from the dead,
ascended to heaven, sat down at the right hand of the
Father,
from where he will come to judge the living and the
dead;
at whose coming all men will rise again with their
bodies
and will give an account for their own actions,
and those who have done good will go into life
everlasting
and those who have done evil into everlasting fire.
This is the catholic faith
which, if anyone does not believe it faithfully and
firmly, he cannot be saved.

[*This modern translation from the Latin is by The Rev.
Roger Beckwith of Latimer House, Oxford, and is used with
permission.*]

Appendix 2:
The profession of faith of Paul VI (1968)

We believe in one God, Father, Son and Holy Spirit, creator of things visible — such as this world in which our brief life runs its course — and of things invisible — such as the pure spirits which are also called angels — and creator in each man of his spiritual and immortal soul.

We believe that this only God is as absolutely one in His infinitely Holy essence as in His other perfections: in His almighty power, His infinite knowledge, His providence, His will and His love. He is 'He who is' as He revealed to Moses *(cf. Exod. 3.14 Vulg.)*; He is 'Love', as the apostle John has taught us *(cf. 1 John 4.8)*; so that these two names, Being and Love, express ineffably the same divine essence of Him who has wished to make Himself manifest to us, and who, 'dwelling in unapproachable light' *(1 Tim. 6.16)*, is in Himself above every name and every created thing and every created intellect. God alone can give us right and full knowledge of Himself by revealing Himself as Father, Son and Holy Spirit, in whose eternal life we are by grace called to share, here on earth in the obscurity of faith and after death in eternal light. The mutual bonds which from all eternity constitute the three persons, each of whom is one and the same divine Being, constitute the blessed inmost life of the most Holy God, infinitely beyond all that we can humanly understand. We give thanks, however, to the divine goodness that very many believers can testify with us before men to the unity of God, even though they know not the mystery of the most Holy Trinity.

We believe then in God who eternally begets the Son; we believe in the Son, the Word of God, who is eternally begotten; we believe in the Holy Spirit, the uncreated person who proceeds from the Father and the Son as their eternal love. Thus, in the three divine persons who are 'equally eternal and fully equal' the life and beatitude of God, perfectly one, superabound and are consummated in the supreme excellence and glory proper to the uncreated essence, and always 'both unity in the Trinity and Trinity in the unity must be worshipped'.

We believe in our Lord Jesus Christ, the Son of God. He is the eternal Word, born of the Father before all ages and of one same substance with the Father, that is one in being with the Father, through Him all things were made. He became flesh from the Virgin Mary by the Holy Spirit and was made man. Therefore, he is 'equal to the Father as to His divinity, less than the Father as to His humanity', entirely one 'not by a confusion of substance' (which is impossible), 'but by the unity of personhood'.

He dwelled among us, full of grace and truth. He proclaimed and established the Kingdom of God, making the Father manifest to us. He gave us His new commandment to love one another as He Himself loved us. He taught us the way of the beatitudes of the Gospel: poverty in spirit, meekness, suffering borne with patience, thirst after justice, mercy, purity of heart, peacemaking, persecution suffered for justice sake. He suffered under Pontius Pilate, He, the Lamb of God bearing the sins of the world; He died for us, nailed to the cross, saving us by His redeeming blood. He was buried and, of His own power, rose again on the third day, raising us by His resurrection to that sharing in the divine life which is the life of grace. He ascended into heaven, wherefrom He shall come again, this time in glory, to judge the living and the dead, each according to his merits: those who have responded to the love and goodness of God will go to eternal life, but those who have rejected them to the end will be sentenced to the fire that will never be extinguished. And to His Kingdom there will be no end.

We believe in the Holy Spirit, the Lord and Giver of life, who together with the Father and the Son is worshipped and glorified. He has spoken through the prophets; He was sent to us by Christ after His resurrection and His ascension to the Father; He enlightens, vivifies, protects and guides the Church; He purifies her members if they do not refuse His grace. His action, which penetrates to the inmost of the soul, enables man to respond to the command of Jesus: 'You must be perfect as your heavenly Father is perfect' *(Matt. 5.48)*.

We believe that Mary, who remained ever a Virgin, is the Mother of the Incarnate Word, our God and Saviour Jesus Christ and that, by reason of her singular election, 'she was, in consideration of the merits of her Son, redeemed in a more eminent manner' 'preserved immune from all stain of original sin', and 'by an exceptional gift of grace stands far above all other creatures.'

Joined by a close and indissoluble bond to the mysteries of the incarnation and redemption, the Blessed Virgin Mary, the Immaculate, 'when the course of her earthly life was finished, was taken up, body and soul, to the glory of heaven' and, likened to her Son who rose again from the dead, she received in anticipation the future lot of all the just. We believe that the Holy Mother of God, the new Eve, 'Mother of the Church' 'continues in heaven to exercise her maternal role' with regard to Christ's members, 'helping to bring forth and to increase the divine life in the souls of all the redeemed'.

We believe that in Adam all have sinned, which means that the original offence committed by him caused the human race, common to all, to fall to a state in which it bears the consequences of that offence. This is no longer the state in which the human natture was at the beginning in our first parents, constituted as they were in holiness and justice, and in which man was immune from evil and death. And so, it is human nature so fallen, deprived from the gift of grace with which it had first been adorned, injured in its own natural powers and subjected to the dominion of death, that is communicated to all men; it is in this sense that every man is born in sin. We therefore hold, with the Council of Trent, that original sin is transmitted with human nature 'by propagation, not by imitation' and that it 'is in all men proper to each'.

We believe that our Lord Jesus Christ by the sacrifice of the Cross redeemed us from original sin and all the personal sins committed by each one of us, so that the word of the apostle is verified: 'Where sin increased grace abounded all the more' (*Rom. 5.20*).

We believe in and confess one baptism instituted by our Lord Jesus Christ for the forgiveness of sins. Baptism should be administered even to little children 'who of themselves cannot have yet committed any sin', in order that, though born deprived of supernatural grace, they may be reborn 'of water and the Holy Spirit' to the divine life in Christ Jesus.

We believe in one, Holy, Catholic and apostolic Church, built by Jesus Christ on that rock which is Peter. She is the 'Mystical Body of Christ', at once a visible society 'provided with hierarchical organs' and a 'spiritual community; the Church on earth', the pilgrim People of God here below, and 'the Church filled with heavenly blessings'; 'the germ and the first fruits of the Kingdom of God', through which the work and the sufferings of redemption are continued throughout human history, and which looks with all its strength for the perfect accomplishment it will obtain beyond time in glory. In the course of time, the Lord Jesus Christ forms His Church by means of the sacraments emanating from His fullness. For by these the Church makes her members share in the mystery of the death and resurrection of Jesus Christ, through the grace of the Holy Spirit who gives her life and movement. She is therefore holy, though having sinners in her midst, because she herself has no other life but the life of grace. If they live by her life, her members are sanctified; if they move away from her life, they fall into sins and disorders that prevent the radiation of her sanctity. This is why she suffers and does penance for those offences, of which she has the power to free her children through the blood of Christ and the gift of the Holy Spirit.

Heiress of the divine promises and daughter of Abraham according to the Spirit, through that Israel whose sacred Scriptures she lovingly guards, and whose patriarchs and prophets she venerates; founded upon the apostles and faithfully handing down through the centuries their everliving word and their powers as pastors in the successor of Peter and the bishops in communion with him; perpetually assisted by the Holy Spirit, the Church has the charge of guarding, teaching, explaining and spreading the truth which God revealed dimly to men through the prophets, and then fully in Lord Jesus. We believe all 'that is contained in the word of God, written or handed down, and that the Church proposes for belief as divinely revealed, whether by a solemn decree or by the ordinary and universal teaching office'. We believe in the infallibility enjoyed by the successor of Peter when, as pastor and teacher of all the Christians, 'he speaks *ex cathedra*' and which 'also resides in the episcopal Body when it exercises with him the supreme teaching office'.

We believe that the Church founded by Jesus Christ and for which He prayed is indefectibly one in faith, worship and the bond of hierarchical communion. In the bosom of this Church, the rich variety of liturgical rites and the legitimate diversity of theological and spiritual heritages and of special disciplines, far from 'injuring her unity, make it more manifest'.

Recognising also the existence, 'outside the organism' of the Church of Christ of 'numerous elements of sanctification and truth which, because they belong to her as her own, call for Catholic unity' and believing in the action of the Holy Spirit who stirs up on the heart of all the disciples of Christ a desire for this unity, we entertain the hope that the Christians who do not yet enjoy full communion in only one Church will at last be united in one flock with only one Shepherd.

We believe that 'the Church is necessary for salvation. For, Christ, who is the sole Mediator and the one way to salvation, makes Himself present for us in His Body which is the Church.' But the divine design of salvation embraces all men; and those 'who without fault on their part do not know the Gospel of Christ and His Church but seek God with a sincere heart, and under the influence of grace endeavour to do His will as recognised through the promptings of their conscience', they too in a number known only to God 'can obtain eternal salvation.'

We believe that the Mass, celebrated by the priest representing the person of Christ by virtue of the power received through the sacrament of Order, and offered by him in the name of Christ and of the members of His Mystical Body, is indeed the sacrifice of Calvary rendered sacramentally present on our altars. We believe that, as the bread and wine consecrated by the Lord at the Last Supper were changed into His body and His blood which were soon to be offered for us on the Cross, likewise the bread and wine consecrated by the priest are changed into the body and blood of Christ enthroned gloriously in heaven; and we believe that the mysterious presence of the Lord, under the species which continue to appear to our senses as before, is a true, real and substantial presence.

Thus, in this sacrament Christ cannot become present otherwise than by the change of the whole substance of bread into His body, and the change of the whole substance of wine into His blood, while only the properties of the bread and wine which our senses perceive remain unchanged. This mysterious change is fittingly and properly named by the Church transubstantiation. Every theological explanation which seeks some understanding of this mystery must, in order to be in accord with Catholic faith maintain firmly that in the order of reality itself, independently of our mind, the bread and wine have ceased to exist after the consecration, so that it is the adorable body and blood of the Lord Jesus which from then on are really before us under the sacramental species of bread and wine, as the Lord willed it, in order to give Himself to us as food and to bind us together in the unity of His Mystical Body.

The unique and indivisible existence of the Lord glorious in heaven is not multiplied, but is rendered present by the sacrament in the many places on earth where the eucharistic sacrifice is celebrated. And this existence remains present, after the celebration of the sacrifice, in the Blessed Sacrament which is, in the tabernacle, as the living heart of our churches. Therefore, it is our sweet duty to honour and adore, in the Blessed Host which our eyes see, the Incarnate Word Himself whom they cannot see and who, yet, without leaving heaven, is made present before us.

We confess also that the Kingdom of God, begun here on earth in the Church of Christ, is not 'of this world' (*John 18.36*) whose 'form is passing away' (*1 Cor. 7.31*), and that its proper growth cannot be identified with the progress of civilisation, of science or of human technology, but that it consists in an ever more profound knowledge of the unfathomable riches of Christ, an ever stronger hope of eternal blessings, an ever more ardent response to the love of God, and finally in an ever more abundant diffusion of grace and holiness among men. But it is this same love which impels the Church to be also continuously concerned about the true temporal welfare of men. While she never ceases to remind all her children that 'they have not' here on earth 'a lasting city' (*Heb. 13.14*), she also urges them to contribute, each according to his condition of life and his means, to the welfare of their earthly city, to promote justice, peace and fraternal concord among men, to give their help generously to their brothers, especially to the poorest and most unfortunate. The deep solicitude of the Church, the Spouse of Christ, for the needs of men, for their joys and hopes, their griefs and efforts, is therefore nothing other

135

than the desire which strongly urges her to be present to them in order to enlighten them with the light of Christ and to gather and unite them all in Him, their only Saviour. This solicitude can never be understood to mean that the Church conforms herself to the things of this world or that the ardour is lessened with which she expects her Lord and the eternal Kingdom.

We believe in the life eternal. We believe that the souls of all those who die in the grace of Christ — whether they must still be purified in purgatory, or, from the moment they leave their bodies, Jesus takes them to paradise as He did for the good thief — constitute the People of God beyond death; death will be finally vanquished on the day of the resurrection when these souls will be re-united with their bodies.

We believe that the multitude of those gathered around Jesus and Mary in paradise forms the Church of heaven, where in the enjoyment of eternal beatitude they see God as He is (1 John 3.2), and where they also, in different ways and degrees, are associated with the holy angels, in the divine rule exercised by the glorified Christ, by interceding for us and by providing with their brotherly solicitude a powerful help to our infirmity.

We believe in the communion of all the faithful of Christ, those who are pilgrims on earth, the dead who are being purified, and the blessed in heaven, all together forming one Church; and we also believe that in this communion the merciful love of God and His saints is ever turning listening ears to our prayers, as Jesus told us: 'Ask and you will receive' (John 16.24). Confessing this faith and sustained by this hope, we look forward to the resurrection of the dead and the life of the world to come.

Blessed be God thrice Holy. Amen.

[This translation of the Latin is from *The Christian Faith in The Doctrinal Documents of the Catholic Church*, (ed. J. Neuner S.J. & J. Dupuis S.J. Bangalore, India, 1973) and used with permission]

Appendix 3:
The Lausanne Covenant (1974)

Introduction

We, members of the Church of Jesus Christ, from more than 150 nations, participants in the International Congress On World Evangelization at Lausanne, praise God for his great salvation and rejoice in the fellowship he has given us with himself and with each other. We are deeply stirred by what God is doing in our day, moved to penitence by our failures and challenged by the unfinished task of evangelization. We believe the gospel is God's good news for the whole world, and we are determined by his grace to obey Christ's commission to proclaim it to all mankind and to make disciples of every nation. We desire, therefore, to affirm our faith and our resolve, and to make public our covenant.

1. The purpose of God

We affirm our belief in the one eternal God, Creator and Lord of the world, Father, Son and Holy Spirit, who governs all things according to the purpose of his will. He has been calling out from the world a people for himself, and sending his people back into the world to be his servants and his witnesses, for the extension of his kingdom, the building up of Christ's body, and the glory of his name. We confess with shame that we have often denied our calling and failed in our mission, by becoming conformed to the world or by withdrawing from it. Yet we rejoice that even when borne by earthen vessels the gospel is still a precious treasure. To the task of making that treasure known in the power of the Holy Spirit we desire to dedicate ourselves anew.

(Isa. 40:28; Matt. 28:19; Eph. 1:11; Acts 15:14; John 17:6, 18; Eph. 4:12; I Cor. 5:10; Rom. 12:2; II Cor. 4:7)

2. The authority and power of the Bible

We affirm the divine inspiration, truthfulness and authority of both Old and New Testament Scriptures in their entirety as the only written word of God, without error in all that it affirms, and the only infallible rule of faith and practice. We also affirm the power of God's word to accomplish his purpose of salvation. The message of the Bible is addressed to all mankind. For God's revelation in Christ and in Scripture is unchangeable. Through it the Holy Spirit still speaks today. He illumines the minds of God's people in every culture to perceive its truth freshly through their own eyes and thus discloses to the whole church ever more of the many-coloured wisdom of God.

(II Tim. 3:16; II Pet. 1:21; John 10:35; Isa. 55:11; I Cor. 1:21; Rom. 1:16; Matt. 5:17, 18; Jude 3; Eph. 1:17, 18; 3:10, 18)

3. The uniqueness and universality of Christ

We affirm that there is only one Saviour and only one gospel, although there is a wide diversity of evangelistic approaches. We recognize that all men have some knowledge of God through his general revelation in nature. But we deny that this can save, for men suppress the truth by their unrighteousness. We also reject as derogatory to Christ and the gospel every kind of syncretism and dialogue which implies that Christ speaks equally through all religions and ideologies. Jesus Christ, being himself the only God-man, who gave himself as the only ransom for sinners, is the only mediator between God and man. There is no other name by which we must

be saved. All men are perishing because of sin, but God loves all men, not wishing that any should perish but that all should repent. Yet those who reject Christ repudiate the joy of salvation and condemn themselves to eternal separation from God. To proclaim Jesus as 'the Saviour of the world' is not to affirm that all men are either automatically or ultimately saved, still less to affirm that all religions offer salvation in Christ. Rather it is to proclaim God's love for a world of sinners and to invite all men to respond to him as Saviour and Lord in the wholehearted personal commitment of repentance and faith. Jesus Christ has been exalted above every other name; we long for the day when every knee shall bow to him and every tongue shall confess him Lord.
(Gal. 1:6–9; Rom. 1:18–32; I Tim. 2:5, 6; Acts 4:12; John 3:16–19; II Pet. 3:9; II Thess. 1:7–9; John 4:42; Matt. 11:28; Eph. 1:20, 21; Phil. 2:9–11)

4. The nature of evangelism

To evangelize is to spread the good news that Jesus Christ died for our sins and was raised from the dead according to the Scriptures, and that as the reigning Lord he now offers the forgiveness of sins and the liberating gift of the Spirit to all who repent and believe. Our Christian presence in the world is indispensable to evangelism, and so is that kind of dialogue whose purpose is to listen sensitively in order to understand. But evangelism itself is the proclamation of the historical, biblical Christ as Saviour and Lord, with a view to persuading people to come to him personally and so be reconciled to God. In issuing the gospel invitation we have no liberty to conceal the cost of discipleship. Jesus still calls all who would follow him to deny themselves, take up their cross, and identify themselves with his new community. The results of evangelism include obedience to Christ, incorporation into his church and responsible service in the world.
(I Cor. 15:3, 4; Acts 2:32–39; John 20:21; I Cor. 1:23; II

Cor. 4, 5; 5:11, 20; Luke 14:25–33; Mark 8:34; Acts 2:40, 47; Mark 10:43–45)

5. Christian social responsibility

We affirm that God is both the Creator and the Judge of all men. We therefore should share his concern for justice and reconciliation throughout human society and for the liberation of men from every kind of oppression. Because mankind is made in the image of God, every person, regardless of race, religion, colour, culture, class, sex or age, has an intrinsic dignity because of which he should be respected and served, not exploited. Here too we express penitence both for our neglect and for having sometimes regarded evengelism and social concern as mutually exclusive. Although reconciliation with man is not reconciliation with God, nor is social action evangelism, nor is political liberation salvation, nevertheless we affirm that evangelism and socio-political involvement are both part of our Christian duty. For both are necessary expressions of our doctrines of God and man, our love for our neighbour and our obedience to Jesus Christ. The message of salvation implies also a message of judgment upon every form of alienation, oppression and discrimination, and we should not be afraid to denounce evil and injustice wherever they exist. When people receive Christ they are born again into his kingdom and must seek not only to exhibit but also to spread its righteousness in the midst of an unrighteous world. The salvation we claim should be transforming us in the totality of our personal and social responsibilities. Faith without works is dead.
(Acts 17:26, 31; Gen. 18:25; Isa. 1:17; Psa. 45:7; Gen. 1:26, 27; Jas. 3:9; Lev. 19:18; Luke 6:27, 35; Jas. 2:14–26; John 3:3, 5; Matt. 5:20; 6:33; II Cor. 3:18; Jas. 2:20)

6. The Church and evangelism

We affirm that Christ sends his redeemed people into the world as the Father sent him, and that this calls for a similar deep and costly penetration of the world. We need to break out of our ecclesiastical ghettos and permeate non-Christian society. In the church's mission of sacrificial service evangelism is primary. World evangelization requires the whole church to take the whole gospel to the whole world. The church is at the very centre of God's cosmic purpose and is his appointed means of spreading the gospel. But a church which preaches the cross must itself be marked by the cross. It becomes a stumbling block to evangelism when it betrays the gospel or lacks a living faith in God, a genuine love for people, or scrupulous honesty in all things including promotion and finance. The church is the community of God's people rather than an institution, and must not be identified with any particular culture, social or political system, or human ideology.
(John 17:18; 20:21; Matt. 28:19, 20; Acts 1:8; 20:27; Eph. 1:9, 10; 3:9–11; Gal. 6:14, 17; II Cor. 6:3, 4; II Tim. 2:19–21; Phil. 1:27)

7. Cooperation in evangelism

We affirm that the church's visible unity in truth is God's purpose. Evangelism also summons us to unity, because our oneness strengthens our witness, just as our disunity undermines our gospel of reconciliation. We recognize, however, that organizational unity may take many forms and does not necessarily forward evangelism. Yet we who share the same biblical faith should be closely united in fellowship, work and witness. We confess that our testimony has sometimes been marred by sinful individualism and needless duplication. We pledge ourselves to seek a deeper unity in truth, worship, holiness and mission. We urge the development of regional and functional cooperation for the furtherance of the church's mission, for strategic planning, for mutual encouragement, and for the sharing of resources and experience. (John 17:21, 23; Eph. 4:3, 4; John 13:35; Phil. 1:27; John 17:11–23)

8. Churches in evangelistic partnership

We rejoice that a new missionary era has dawned. The dominant role of western missions is fast disappearing. God is raising up from the younger churches a great new resource for world evangelization, and is thus demonstrating that the responsibility to evangelize belongs to the whole body of Christ. All churches should therefore be asking God and themselves what they should be doing both to reach their own area and to send missionaries to other parts of the world. A re-evaluation of our missionary responsibility and role should be continuous. Thus a growing partnership of churches will develop and the universal character of Christ's church will be more clearly exhibited. We also thank God for agencies which labour in Bible translation, theological education, the mass media, Christian literature, evangelism, missions, church renewal and other specialist fields. They too should engage in constant self-examination to evaluate their effectiveness as part of the Church's mission. (Rom. 1:8; Phil. 1:5; 4:15; Acts 13:1–3; I Thess. 1:6–8)

9. The urgency of the evangelistic task

More than 2,700 million people, which is more than two-thirds of mankind, have yet to be evangelized. We are ashamed that so many have been neglected; it is a standing rebuke to us and to the whole church. There is now, however, in many parts of the world an unprecedented receptivity to the Lord Jesus Christ. We are convinced that this is the time for churches and para-church agencies to pray earnestly for the salvation of the unreached and to launch new efforts to achieve world evangelization. A reduction of foreign missionaries and

money in an evangelized country may sometimes be necessary to facilitate the national church's growth in self-reliance and to release resources for unevangelized areas. Missionaries should flow ever more freely from and to all six continents in a spirit of humble service. The goal should be, by all available means and at the earliest possible time, that every person will have the opportunity to hear, understand, and receive the good news. We cannot hope to attain this goal without sacrifices. All of us are shocked by the poverty of millions and disturbed by the injustices which cause it. Those of us who live in affluent circumstances accept our duty to develop a simple life-style in order to contribute more generously to both relief and evangelism.
(John 9;4; Matt. 9;35–38; Rom. 9:1–3; I Cor. 9:19–23; Mark 16:15; Isa. 58:6, 7; Jas. 1:27; 2:1–9; Matt. 25:31–46; Acts 2:44, 45; 4:34, 35)

10. Evangelism and culture

The development of strategies for world evangelization calls for imaginative pioneering methods. Under God, the result will be the rise of churches deeply rooted in Christ and closely related to their culture. Culture must always be tested and judged by Scripture. Because man is God's creature, some of his culture is rich in beauty and goodness. Because he has fallen, all of it is tainted with sin and some of it is demonic. The gospel does not presuppose the superiority of any culture to another, but evaluates all cultures according to its own criteria of truth and righteousness, and insists on moral absolutes in every culture. Missions have all too frequently exported with the gospel an alien culture, and churches have sometimes been in bondage to culture rather than to the Scripture. Christ's evangelists must humbly seek to empty themselves of all but their personal authenticity in order to become the servants of others, and churches must seek to transform and enrich culture, all for the glory of God.

(Mark 7:8, 9, 13; Gen. 4:21, 22; I Cor. 9:19–23; Phil. 2:5–7; II Cor. 4:5)

11. Education and leadership

We confess that we have sometimes pursued church growth at the expense of church depth, and divorced evangelism from Christian nurture. We also acknowledge that some of our missions have been too slow to equip and encourage national leaders to assume their rightful responsibilities. Yet we are committed to indigenous principles, and long that every church will have national leaders who manifest a Christian style of leadership in terms not of domination but of service. We recognize that there is a great need to improve theological education, especially for church leaders. In every nation and culture there should be an effective training programme for pastors and laymen in doctrine, discipleship, evangelism, nurture and service. Such training programmes should not rely on any stereotyped methodology but should be developed by creative local initiatives according to biblical standards.
(Col. 1:27, 28; Acts 14:23; Tit. 1:5, 9; Mark 10:42–45; Eph. 4:11, 12)

12. Spiritual conflict

We believe that we are engaged in constant spiritual warfare with the principalities and powers of evil, who are seeking to overthrow the church and frustrate its task of world evangelization. We know our need to equip ourselves with God's armour and to fight this battle with the spiritual weapons of truth and prayer. For we detect the activity of our enemy, not only in false ideologies outside the church, but also inside it in false gospels which twist Scripture and put man in the place of God. We need both watchfulness and discernment to safeguard the biblical gospel. We acknowledge that we ourselves are not immune to wordliness of thought and action, that is, to a surrender to secularism. For example, although careful studies of church growth, both numerical and spiritual, are right and valuable, we have sometimes neglected them. At other times, desirous to ensure a response to the gospel, we have compromised our message, manipulated our hearers through pressure techniques, and become unduly preoccupied with statistics or even dishonest in our use of them. All this is worldly. The church must be in the world; the world must not be in the church.

(Eph. 6:12; II Cor. 4:3, 4; Eph. 6:11, 13–18; II Cor 10:3–5; I John 2:18–26, 4:1–3; Gal. 1:6–9; II Cor. 2:17. 4:2; John 17:15)

13. Freedom and persecution

It is the God-appointed duty of every government to secure conditions of peace, justice and liberty in which the church may obey God, serve the Lord Christ, and preach the gospel without interference. We therefore pray for the leaders of the nations and call upon them to guarantee freedom of thought and conscience, and freedom to practise and propagate religion in accordance with the will of God and as set forth in *The Universal Declaration of Human Rights*. We also express our deep concern for all who have been unjustly imprisoned, and especially for our brethren who are suffering for their testimony to the Lord Jesus. We promise to pray and work for their freedom. At the same time we refuse to be intimidated by their fate. God helping us, we too will seek to stand against injustice and to remain faithful to the gospel, whatever the cost. We do not forget the warnings of Jesus that persecution is inevitable.

(I Tim. 1:1–4; Acts 4:19, 5:29; Col. 3:24; Heb. 13:1–3; Luke 4:18; Gal. 5:11, 6:12; Matt. 5:10–12; John 15:18–21)

14. The power of the Holy Spirit

We believe in the power of the Holy Spirit. The Father sent his Spirit to bear witness to his Son; without his witness ours is futile. Conviction of sin, faith in Christ, new birth and Christian growth are all his work. Further, the Holy Spirit is a missionary spirit; thus evangelism will become a realistic possibility only when the Spirit renews the church in truth and wisdom, faith, holiness, love and power. We therefore call upon all Christians to pray for such a visitation of the sovereign Spirit of God that all his fruit may appear in all his people and that all his gifts may enrich the body of Christ. Only then will the whole church become a fit instrument in his hands, that the whole earth may hear his voice.

(I Cor. 2:4; John 15:26, 27; 16:8–11; I Cor. 12:3; John 3:6–8; II Cor. 3:18; John 7:37–39; I Thess. 5:19; Acts 1:8; Psa. 85:4–7, 67:1–3; Gal. 5:22, 23; I Cor. 12:4–31; Rom. 12:3–8)

15. The return of Christ

We believe that Jesus Christ will return personally and visibly, in power and glory, to consummate his salvation and his judgment. This promise of his coming is a further spur to our evangelism, for we remember his words that the gospel must first be preached to all nations. We believe that the interim period between Christ's ascension and return is to be filled with the mission of the people of God, who have no liberty to stop before the End. We also remember his warning that false Christs and false prophets will arise as precursors of the final Antichrist. We therefore reject as a proud, selfconfident dream the notion that man can ever build a utopia on earth. Our Christian confidence is that God will perfect his kingdom, and we look forward with eager anticipation to that day, and to the new heaven and earth in which righteousness will dwell and God will reign for ever. Meanwhile, we rededicate ourselves to the service

of Christ and of men in joyful submission to his authority over the whole of our lives.
(Mark 14:62; Heb. 9:28; Mark 13:10; Acts 1:8–11; Matt. 28:20; Mark 13:21–23; John 2:18, 4:1–3; Luke 12:32; Rev. 21:1–5; II Pet. 3:13; Matt. 28:18)

Conclusion

Therefore, in the light of this our faith and our resolve, we enter into a solemn covenant with God and with each other, to pray, to plan and to work together for the evangelization of the whole world. We call upon others to join us. May God help us by his grace and for his glory to be faithful to this our covenant! Amen, Alleluia!

Note: In 1982 the Lausanne Committee for World Evangelization published a further statement, *Evangelism and Social Responsibility, An Evangelical Commitment.*

Appendix 4:
A letter to a Roman Catholic

by
John Wesley

(Originally published in Dublin as a tract in 1749, this **Letter** *went through several editions. In the context of the great bitterness which then existed in Ireland between Roman Catholics and Protestants, the content reveals a true catholic spirit.)*

1. You have heard ten thousand stories of us who are commonly called Protestants, of which, if you believe only one in a thousand, you must think very hardly of us. But this is quite contrary to our Lord's rule, 'judge not, that ye be not judged' (Matt. 7:1), and has many ill consequences, particularly this: it inclines us to think as hardly of you. Hence, we are on both sides less willing to help one another and more ready to hurt each other. Hence brotherly love is utterly destroyed and each side, looking on the other as monsters, gives way to anger, hatred, malice, to every unkind affection — which have frequently broke out in such inhuman barbarities as are scarce named even among the heathens.

2. Now can nothing be done, even allowing us on both sides to retain our own opinions, for the softening our hearts towards each other, the giving a check to this flood of unkindness and restoring at least some small degree of love among our neighbours and countrymen? Do not you wish for this? Are you not fully convinced that malice, hatred, revenge, bitterness (whether in us or in you, in our hearts or yours) are an abomination to the Lord (*cf.*

Prov. 15:26; 16:5)? Be our opinions right or be they wrong, these tempers are undeniably wrong. They are the broad road that leads to destruction, to the nethermost hell.

3. I do not suppose all the bitterness is on your side. I know there is too much on our side also. So much that I fear many Protestants (so-called) will be angry at me, too, for writing to you in this manner, and will say, ' 'Tis showing you too much favour; you deserve no such treatment at our hands.'

4. But I think you do. I think you deserve the tenderest regard I can show, were it only because the same God hath raised you and me from the dust of the earth and has made us both capable of loving and enjoying him to eternity; were it only because the Son of God has bought you and me with his own blood. How much more, if you are a person fearing God (as without question many of you are) and studying to have a conscience void of offence towards God and towards man?

5. I shall therefore endeavour, as mildly and inoffensively as I can, to remove in some measure the ground of your unkindness by plainly declaring what our belief and what our practice is: that you may see we are not altogether such monsters as perhaps you imagined us to be.

A true Protestant may express his belief in these or the like words:

6. As I am assured that there is an infinite and independent Being and that it is impossible there should be more than one, so I believe that this one God is the Father of all things, especially of angels and men; that he is in a peculiar manner the Father of those whom he regenerates by his Spirit, whom he adopts in his Son as co-heirs with him and crowns with an eternal inheritance; but in a still higher sense, the Father of his only Son, whom he hath begotten from eternity.

I believe this Father of all not only to be able to do whatsoever pleaseth him but also to have an eternal right of making what and when and how he pleaseth; and of possessing and disposing of all that he has made; and that he of his own goodness created heaven and earth, and all that is therein.

7. I believe that Jesus of Nazareth was the Saviour of the world, the Messiah so long foretold; that, being anointed with the Holy Ghost, he was a *prophet*, revealing to use the whole will of God; that he was a *priest*, who gave himself a sacrifice for sin, and still makes intercession for transgressors; that he is a *king*, who has all power in heaven and in earth, and will reign till he has subdued all things to himself (*cf.* 1 Cor. 15:27–28).

I believe he is the proper, natural Son of God, God of God, very God of very God; and that he is the Lord of all, having absolute, supreme universal dominion over all things; but more peculiarly *our* Lord (who believe in him), both by conquest, purchase, and voluntary obligation.

I believe that he was made man, joining the human nature with the divine in one person, being conceived by the singular operation of the Holy Ghost and born of the Blessed Virgin Mary, who, as well after as she brought him forth, continued a pure and unspotted virgin.

I believe he suffered inexpressible pains both of body and soul and at last death, even the death of the cross (*cf.* Phil. 2:8), at the time that Pontius Pilate governed Judea under the Roman Emperor; that his body was then laid in the grave and his soul went to the place of separate spirits; that the third day he rose again from the dead; that he ascended into heaven, where he remains in the midst of the throne of God in the highest power and glory as Mediator till the end of the world, as God to all eternity; that, in the end, he will come down from heaven to judge every man according to his works, both those who shall be then alive and all who have died before that day.

8. I believe the infinite and eternal Spirit of God, equal with the Father and the Son, to be not only perfectly holy in himself, but the immediate cause of all

holiness in us: enlightening our understandings, rectifying our wills and affections, renewing our natures, uniting our persons to Christ, assuring us of the adoption of sons, leading us in our actions, purifying and sanctifying our souls and bodies to a full and eternal enjoyment of God.

9. I believe that Christ and his Apostles gathered unto himself a church to which he has continually added such as shall be saved; that this catholic (that is, universal) Church, extending to all nations and all ages, is holy in all its members, who have fellowship with God the Father, Son and Holy Ghost; that they have fellowship with the holy angels who constantly minister to these heirs of salvation, and with all the living members of Christ on earth, as well as all who are departed [this life] in his faith and fear.

10. I believe God forgives all the sins of them that truly repent and unfeignedly believe his holy gospel; and that, at the last day, all men shall arise again, every one with his own body.

I believe that, as the unjust shall after their resurrection be tormented in hell for ever, so the just shall enjoy inconceivable happiness in the presence of God to all eternity.

11. Now, is there anything wrong in this? Is there any one point which you do not believe as well as we?

But you think we ought to believe more? We will not now enter into the dispute. Only let me ask: 'If a man sincerely believes thus much and practices accordingly, can any one possibly persuade you to think that such a man shall perish everlastingly?'

12. 'But does he practise accordingly?' If he does not, we grant all his faith will not save him. And this leads me to show you in few and plain words, what the practice of a true Protestant is. I say 'a true Protestant,' for I disclaim all common swearers, Sabbath-breakers, drunkards, all whoremongers, liars, cheats, extortioners — in a word, all that live in open sin. These are no Protestants; they are no Christians at all. Give them their own name:

they are open heathens. They are the curse of the nation, the bane of society, the shame of mankind, the scum of the earth.

13. A true Protestant believes in God, has a full confidence in his mercy, fears him with a filial fear, and loves him with all his soul. He worships God in spirit and in truth, in every thing gives him thanks, calls upon him with his heart as well as his lips, at all times and in all places, honours his holy Name and his Word and serves him truly all the days of his life.

Now, do not you yourself approve of this? Is there any one point you can condemn? Do not you practise as well as approve of it? Can you ever be happy if you do not? Can you ever expect true peace in this, or glory in the world to come, if you do not believe in God through Christ, if you do not thus fear and love God? My dear friend, consider: I am not persuading you to leave or change your religion, but to follow after that fear and love of God without which all religion is vain. I say not a word to you about your opinions or outward manner of worship. But I say, all worship is an abomination to the Lord unless you worship him in spirit and in truth, with your heart as well as your lips, with your spirit and with your understanding also (*cf.* 1 Cor. 14:15). Be your form of worship what it will, but in every thing give him thanks; else it is all but lost labour. Use whatever outward observances you please, but put your whole trust in him, but honour his holy Name and his Word, and serve him truly all the days of your life.

14. Again: a true Protestant loves his neighbour (that is, every man, friend or enemy, good or bad) as himself, as he loves his own soul, as Christ loved us. And as Christ laid down his life for us, so is he ready to lay down his life for his brethren. He shows this love by doing to all men in all points as he would they should do unto him. He loves, honours, and obeys his father and mother and helps them to the uttermost of his power. He honours and obeys the king and all that are put in authority under him. He cheerfully submits to all his governors, teachers,

spiritual pastors and masters. He behaves lowly and reverently to all his betters. He hurts nobody, by word or deed. He is true and just in all his dealings. He bears no malice or hatred in his heart. He abstains from all evil-speaking, lying and slandering, neither is guile found in his mouth. Knowing his body to be the temple of the Holy Ghost (*cf.* 1 Cor. 3:16), he keeps it in sobriety, temperance and chastity. He does not desire other men's goods, but is content with that he hath, labours to get his own living and to do the whole will of God in that state of life unto which it has pleased God to call him.

15. Have you any thing to reprove in this? Are you not herein even as he? If not (tell the truth), are you not condemned both by God and your own conscience? Can you fall short of any one point hereof without falling short of being a Christian?

Come, my brother, and let us reason together. Are you right if you only love your friend and hate your enemy? Do not even the heathens and publicans so (*cf.* Matt. 5:43–46)? You are called to love your enemies, to bless them that curse you and to pray for them that despitefully use you and persecute you. But are you not disobedient to the heavenly calling (*cf.* Acts 26:19)? Does your tender love to all men, not only the good but also the evil and unthankful, approve you the child of your Father which is in heaven? Otherwise, whatever you believe and whatever you practice, you are of your father the devil. Are you ready to lay down your life for your brethren? And do you do unto all as you would they should do unto you? If not, do not deceive your own soul: you are but a heathen still. Do you love, honour and obey your father and mother, and help them to the utmost of your power? Do you honour and obey all in authority, all your governors, spiritual pastors and masters? Do you behave lowly and reverently to all your betters? Do you hurt nobody, by word or deed? Are you true and just in all your dealings? Do you take care to pay whatever you owe? Do you feel no malice, or envy or revenge, no hatred or bitterness to any man? If you do, it is plain you are not of God, for all these are the tempers of the devil. Do you speak the truth from your heart to all men, and that in tenderness and love? Are you an Israelite indeed, in whom is no guile (*cf.* John 1:47)? Do you keep your body in sobriety, temperance and chastity, as knowing it is the temple of the Holy Ghost and that, if any man defile the temple of God, him will God destroy (*cf.* 1 Cor. 3:17)? Have you learned in every state wherein you are, therewith to be content? Do you labour to get your own living, abhorring idleness as you abhor hell-fire? The devil tempts other men, but an idle man tempts the devil. An idle man's brain is the devil's shop, where he is continually working mischief. Are you not slothful in business? Whatever your hand finds to do, do you do it with your might? And do you do all as unto the Lord, as a sacrifice unto God, acceptable in Christ Jesus?

This, and this alone, is the old religion. This is true, primitive Christianity. O when shall it spread over all the earth? When shall it be found both in us and you? Without waiting for others, let each of us, by the grace of God, amend one['s own self].

16. Are we not thus far agreed? Let us thank God for this, and receive it as a fresh token of his love. But if God still loveth us, we ought also to love one another. We ought, without this endless jangling about opinions, to provoke one another to love and to good works. Let the points wherein we differ stand aside: here are enough wherein we agree, enough to be the ground of every Christian temper and of every Christian action.

O brethren, let us not still fall out by the way. I hope to see *you* in heaven. And if I practise the religion above described, you dare not say I shall go to hell. You cannot think so. None can persuade you to it. Your own conscience tells you the contrary. Then if we cannot as yet *think alike* in all things, at least we may *love alike*. Herein we cannot possibly do amiss. For of one point none can doubt a moment: God is love; and he that dwelleth in love, dwelleth in God, and God in him [1

John 4:16).

17. In the name, then, and in the strength of God, let us resolve, first, not to hurt one another, to do nothing unkind or unfriendly to each other, nothing which we would not have done to ourselves. Rather let us endeavour after every instance of a kind, friendly and Christian behaviour towards each other.

Let us resolve, secondly, God being our helper, to speak nothing harsh or unkind of each other. The sure way to avoid this is to say all the good we can, both of and to one another; in all our conversation, either with or concerning each other, to use only the language of love; to speak with all softness and tenderness, with the most endearing expression which is consistent with truth and sincerity.

Let us, thirdly, resolve to harbour no unkind thought, no unfriendly temper towards each other. Let us lay the axe to the root of the tree (*cf.* Matt. 3:10), let us examine all that rises in our heart and suffer no disposition there which is contrary to tender affection. Then shall we easily refrain from unkind actions and words, when the very root of bitterness is cut up (*cf.* Heb. 12:15).

Let us, fourthly, endeavour to help each other on in whatever we are agreed leads to the Kingdom. So far as we can, let us always rejoice to strengthen each other's hands in God. Above all, let us each take heed unto himself (since each must give an account of himself to God) that he fall not short of the religion of love; that he be not condemned in that he himself approveth. O let you and me (whatever others do) press on to the prize of our high calling — that, being justified by faith, we may have peace with God through our Lord Jesus Christ; that we may rejoice in God through Jesus Christ, by whom we have received the atonement (*cf.* Rom. 5:1–2); that the love of God may be shed abroad in our hearts by the Holy Ghost which is given unto us (*cf.* Rom. 5:5). Let us count all things but loss for the excellency of the knowledge of Jesus Christ our Lord, being ready for him to suffer the loss of all things and counting them but dung, that we

may win Christ (*cf.* Phil. 3:8).
Dublin

July 18, 1749
(from *Works*, Vol. X, pp. 80–86)

Appendix 5:
The twenty-one Councils

1. NICAEA I (325)
   Condemned Arianism; defined that the Son of God is 'consubstantial' with the Father; formulated the Nicene Creed.
2. CONSTANTINOPLE I (381)
   Condemned the Macedonians, who denied the divinity of the Holy Spirit; confirmed and extended the Nicene Creed.
3. EPHESUS (431)
   Condemned Nestorianism, which held that there were two distinct persons in the Incarnate Christ, a human and divine; defended the right of Mary to be called the Mother of God (*theotokos*).
4. CHALCEDON (451)
   Condemned Monophysitism or Eutychianism, by defining that Christ had two distinct natures, and was therefore true God and true man.
5. CONSTANTINOPLE II (553)
   Pronounced against certain persons as infected with Nestorianism, notably Theodore of Mopsuestia, Theodoret of Cyrrhus and Ibas of Edessa.
6. CONSTANTINOPLE III (680–81)
   Defined, against the Monothelites, that Christ has two wills; human and divine.
7. NICAEA II (787)
   Condemned the Iconoclasts or Image-breakers, and defined that sacred images may be honoured without idolatry.
8. CONSTANTINOPLE IV (869–70)
   Condemned Photius as Patriarch of Constantinople.

9. LATERAN I (1123)
First general council in the West, endorsed the Concordat of Worms regarding the investiture of prelates.

10. LATERAN II (1139)
Took measures against the schism of the antipope Anacletus II and issued disciplinary decrees.

11. LATERAN III (1179)
Legislated against the Waldensians and Albigensians; decreed that papal elections were to be by two-thirds majority of cardinals at conclave.

12. LATERAN IV (1215)
Made reform decrees; ordered the faithful to make annual confession and to receive Easter Communion; first officially used the term 'transubstantiaton'.

13. LYONS I (1245)
Condemned Frederick II for his persecution of the Church.

14. LYONS II (1274)
Effected a temporary reunion of the Eastern Churches with Rome, and decreed that papal elections should begin ten days after the death of the Pope.

15. VIENNE (1311–12)
Suppressed the Knights Templar; sought aid for the Holy Land; defined the relation of the soul to the human body, and condemned the false mysticism of the Fraticelli, Dulcinists, Beghards, and Beguines.

16. CONSTANCE (1414–18)
Issued reform decrees in 'head and members'; condemned John Wyclif and John Hus, and put an end to the Western Schism.

17. FLORENCE (1438–45)
Affirmed the papal primacy against Conciliarists, who said that a general council was superior to the Pope; and sought to effect a reunion of the Eastern Churches separated from Rome.

18. LATERAN V (1512–17)

Defined the relation of Pope to a general council; condemned philosophers who taught the human soul was mortal, with only one soul for all mankind; and called for a crusade against the Turks.

19. TRENT (1545–63)

Called to meet the crisis of the Protestant Reformation; proclaimed the Bible and tradition as rule of faith; defined doctrine of the Mass, the sacraments, justification, purgatory, indulgences, invocation of saints, veneration of sacred images; and issued decrees on marriage and clerical reform.

20. VATICAN I (1869–70)

Defined the nature of revelation and faith, the relation of faith and reason, and papal infallibility; condemned pantheism, materialism, deism, naturalism, and fideism.

21. VATICAN II (1962–65)

Convoked by Pope John XXIII. Its sixteen documents reaffirmed the principles of Roman Catholic faith and morality in a new style; and authorised numerous developments in the Eucharistic liturgy, the ritual of the sacraments, and in the Church's administrative structure.

Bibliography

Collections of Documents used in this study

Abbott W.M., *The Documents of Vatican II* (London 1966).

Bettenson H., *Documents of the Christian Church* (Oxford, 1944)

Cochrane A., *Reformed Confessions of the Sixteenth Century* (London 1966)

Common Prayer, The Book of (1662)

Denzinger H., *Enchiridion Symbolorum* (edition of 1937)

Flannery A., *Vatican Council II: The Conciliar and Post Conciliar Documents* (Leominster, 1975)

Leith J, *Creeds of the Churches* (Richmond, Virginia, 1973)

McGlothin W.J., *Baptist Confessions of Faith* (Boston, Mass., 1911)

Schaff P., *Creeds of Christendom* (3 vols, new ed. Grand Rapids, Mich. 1977)

Stott J., *The Lausanne Covenant* (Minneapolis, Minn., 1975)

Walker W., *The Creeds and Platforms of Congregationalism* (Philadelphia, Penn. 1960)

Also, from the Catholic Truth Society, individual copies of Conciliar Documents, Papal Encyclicals and statements from the various Vatican Congregations (e.g. of Rites).